VATICAN II

The Battle for Meaning

Massimo Faggioli

Paulist Press
New York / Mahwah, NJ

Cover and book design by Sharyn Banks

Library of Congress Cataloging-in-Publication Data

Faggioli, Massimo.
    Vatican II : the battle for meaning / Massimo Faggioli.
        p. cm.
    Includes bibliographical references (p.   ).
    ISBN 978-0-8091-4750-2 (alk. paper) — ISBN 978-1-61643-089-4
1. Vatican Council (2nd : 1962–1965)—History—Congresses. I. Title.
    BX8301962 .F58 2012
    262'.52—dc23

                                                        2011042938

Published by Paulist Press
997 Macarthur Boulevard
Mahwah, New Jersey 07430

www.paulistpress.com

Printed and bound in the
United States of America

CONTENTS

iii

CONTENTS

To our daughter, Laura

ACKNOWLEDGMENTS

The assistance and wisdom of many people contributed immensely to this book; acknowledging this broad network of people is but one, insufficient way to thank them for their tremendous kindness and patience.

I accomplished the first step of this project during my year as a visiting fellow at the Jesuit Institute at Boston College (2008–9), where I had the chance to work in the hospitable environment created by its director, T. Frank Kennedy, SJ. That wonderful year at Boston College laid the foundations for many of the ideas and motivations for writing this book, through the friendly meetings with John Baldovin, SJ; Ken Himes, OFM; Jim Keenan, SJ; Bruce Morrill, SJ; and Stephen Schloesser, SJ. I am particularly grateful to Lisa Cahill, who in 2007 had encouraged me to apply for the fellowship at the Jesuit Institute as a way to begin my American journey. *Vatican II: The Battle for Meaning* is not only about the council; it is also about the scholarship about the council—the debates about the debates—especially after the completion of the five-volume *History of Vatican II* edited by Giuseppe Alberigo and Joseph A. Komonchak.

Leaving my *alma mater studiorum*, Bologna and the "Fondazione per le scienze religiose Giovanni XXIII," in June 2008 did not sever my ties with colleagues and friends there who have been extremely precious. Here I thank in particular Alberto Melloni, Silvia Scatena, and Giovanni Turbanti. A special thank-you to Giuseppe Ruggieri, who as editor of *Cristianesimo nella*

Acknowledgments

Storia hosted the first steps of this meta-narrative about Vatican II in the form of "bibliographical overviews"—an idea among many other ideas that Giuseppe Alberigo had proposed to me during my twelve years in the "Istituto per le scienze religiose" at via San Vitale 114, in Bologna.

During my first two years of teaching at the University of St. Thomas, beginning in September 2009, a number of my colleagues made the completion of this project possible. I am especially grateful to Bernard Brady, chair of the fine theology department, who believed in the research on Vatican II as well as in me; to Michael Hollerich, who eased my entry into a new academic context with kind attentiveness; to Gerard Schlabach, with whom I had the chance to discuss Vatican II over several sushi dinners; to John Boyle, for the *dulcedo societatis* of his Friday afternoon reading group; to Sr. Katarina Schuth, OSF, and Fr. Michael Joncas, precious contact points in the field of scholarship on the relationship between American Catholicism and Vatican II; to the Faculty Development Center at the University of St. Thomas, which supported this project with a generous summer research grant in 2010; and finally, to my undergraduate students at the University of St. Thomas and my graduate students at the Saint Paul Seminary School of Divinity, both indispensable *locus theologicus* for grasping the "joys and hopes" of the theology of Vatican II.

A number of eminent scholars read parts of the manuscript: John O'Malley, SJ, is not only a constant source of encouragement, but also my real "correspondent" during those first years of my American experience and a source of reassurance in delicate moments. Mark Massa, SJ, dean of the School of Theology and Ministry at Boston College, is an inexhaustible source of sage advice (and much-needed good cheer). Jared Wicks, SJ, proved extremely punctual and one of the most demanding readers I have ever had. In addition, in various moments of my research, Peter Hünermann, Joseph Komonchak, Marcello Neri, Gilles Routhier, and Ormond Rush helped me to gain a sense of my footing in the contemporary theological debate.

In the broad network of people who supported this research spiritually and intellectually I cannot forget Thomas Bremer; Dom Emilio Contardi and Msgr. Giuseppe Maria Croce of the Monastery of Camaldoli (Italy); Peter De Mey; Rita Ferrone; Richard Gaillardetz; Anthony Godzieba; Brad Hinze; Thomas Kselman; Nicholas Lash; Gerard Mannion; Timothy Matovina; Sandra Mazzolini; John McGreevy; Serena Noceti; Ladislas Orsy, SJ; Karim Schelkens; David Schultenover, SJ; Kathleen Sprows Cummings; and Maureen Sullivan.

My editor at Paulist Press, Christopher Bellitto, played a crucial role in the conception of this book and in its shaping, thanks not only to his acute editorial skills but also to his scholarly knowledge of the importance of the debate on Vatican II as a historical subject. I consider him not only a colleague, but also a friend who helped me enter and navigate the American university system. Susan Heyboer O'Keefe, my copy editor, was incredibly supportive and patient with my manuscript and me.

Finally, Sarah, my wife, has been unfaltering in her attempt to give a "human face" not only to my English but also to my whole being.

A SHORT HISTORY OF THE DEBATE ON VATICAN II

THE DEBATE ON AN EPOCH-MAKING COUNCIL

Although fifty years have passed since Vatican II began on October 11, 1962—in the *aula* of Saint Peter's in Rome with John XXIII's opening speech, *Gaudet Mater Ecclesia*—from a historical perspective, the council is still very young. The two-thousand-year history of the Church's councils bears witness to a necessarily slow and lengthy reception of every ecumenical council, especially epoch-making councils like the Council of Trent (1545–63) and Vatican II (1962–65). The truly "ecumenical" impact of Vatican II makes the reception of the council even more complex. As a matter of fact, no one disputes the epoch-making impact of Vatican II. The debate sparked in the Catholic Church after the election of Joseph Ratzinger—Benedict XVI (April 19, 2005)—on the hermeneutics of the Second Vatican Council is the strongest evidence for the driving force of the council in the life of the Church, as well as for the risk that the interpretations of the council will drift apart.[1] Proof of the council's central role in the Church's path toward its future in the modern world is that the lively debate on Vatican II—both historical and theological—is far from over, even if the generation of bishops, theologians, and lay men and women active at the time of its celebration is gradually making room for a new generation of Catholics. This new generation is potentially indifferent, dismissive, or even hostile to Vatican II on the basis of a politically oriented presentation of "Vatican II Catholicism" too often labeled "liberal" and "compliant," if not worse.[2] On the other side, the interest about Vatican II seems to be more evident than ever, as demonstrated by the decision of Benedict XVI to put Vatican II on the agenda of the 2010 meeting of his former students—the "Ratzinger Schülerkreis"—at his summer residence in Castel Gandolfo.

This is why it is critical to assess the state of the debate on the council, starting with the debate that took place at Vatican II on the council itself. Fifty years after the council's beginning, the leadership of the Church—the generation of bishops and theologians active at the council—has been replaced. The transmission of the self-representation of Vatican II is crucial to understanding its achievements and shortcomings as they have been debated in the last fifty years.[3] The best way to reflect on the state of Catholicism in the twenty-first-century global world is to regain possession of the event that shaped the Church in a way that is comparable only to the impact of the Council of Trent on European Catholicism. The tangled dimensions of Vatican II, with the rediscovered character of the "catholicity" of the Catholic Church as a "World Church," make the debate on Vatican II rich, culturally and linguistically diversified, politically sensitive, and thus extremely interesting to explore.

One of the effects of the introduction of the 24/7 news cycle in the culture of the Catholic Church is the risk of forgetting the historical depth of the debate on Vatican II, the council's significance, and its reception. Similarly, one of the main outcomes of the activity of the Catholic blogosphere is to simplify and reduce the debate on Vatican II to gossip, or to make theological and historical arguments about the council as arcane and jargon-like as possible—an ironic destiny for a "pastoral council," as John XXIII intended it when he announced it on January 25, 1959. In order to avoid the false impression of a debate driven by the needs of the news cycle or the agenda of some inner circle or particular "school," the first step is to trace the debate back to its origins.

WHAT VATICAN II SAID
ABOUT VATICAN II (1960–65)

John XXIII announced Vatican Council II on January 25, 1959. After a long period preparing the texts to be discussed, between 1962 and 1965 bishops and hundreds of theologians from all over the world assembled for the first time: 2,500 representatives of a Church that had begun to shape herself as a "World Church" from a cultural and theological standpoint. During all of the ecumenical councils from the twelfth century to Vatican Council I (1869–70), the representation of non-European bishops was limited to a tiny symbolic attendance from non-European Catholic Churches.

This new catholicity of the Catholic Church represented at Vatican II was the basic fact that contributed to the early reception of Vatican II by the council itself, that is, by the bishops hailing from local Churches around the world. The fact that Vatican II was the first truly global council is evident not only in the theology of the documents debated and approved (starting with the liturgical constitution *Sacrosanctum Concilium*, approved in December 1963), but also in the reception of these documents.

A decisive element in the passage from a heavily European Catholicism toward a world Catholicism was the contribution of the revival movements in the first decades of the twentieth century. The biblical movement, the liturgical renewal, the patristic revival, and *ressourcement*—a return to the earlier sources of an undivided Church—and the ecumenical movement based in Europe and North America survived the modernist crisis at the beginning of the twentieth century and the condemnations of Pius XII and managed to bring to the fathers and *periti* of Vatican II the core of their historical-theological reflections on the renewal of the Catholic Church. The biblical revival introduced into the Catholic Church the desire for direct access to the Bible for every faithful. The liturgical renewal stressed not only the centrality of the active participation of the faithful, but also the need to reset the balance of the life of the Church around the liturgy and additionally to renew the liturgical language in order to strengthen spiritual life through a development of the principles of adaptation and inculturation with the local cultures of the individual Catholic Churches. The ecumenical movement had suffered some severe setbacks from Rome from the 1920s on, but at the local level it had slowly broken the taboo of exchanges between Catholics, Protestants, and Orthodox Christians. The patristic renewal had advocated a return to the great tradition of the Church fathers (Greek and Latin), a tradition that was more theological and less juridical, and was prior to European Christendom and the myth of an exclusively European Catholicism, especially from a cultural point of view.

Also, thanks to the legacy of these theological movements and to their contribution to the council, Vatican II was not only an assembly that debated on the wording of the final drafts of the documents, but it also became a moment of reflection and not seldom of spiritual and intellectual "conversion" to the need for a real *aggiornamento* for many of its participants. From the very beginning of the preparation of the council, bishops and theologians from European and non-European, non-Western and non-Latin traditions alike started writing private journals and diaries that demonstrate the profound awareness of the event in the heart and minds of the participants. The availability of these documents (some of them have been already published) makes it impossible to deny the fact that the very protagonists of Vatican II lived it as an experience that influenced—sometimes dramatically—their way of conceiving the relationship between the Church and tradition, the Church and culture, and the Church and the modern world.[4]

The institutional mechanics of the council contributed to the growth of this awareness. The first document to be debated and approved by Vatican II (October 1962–November 1963), the liturgical constitution *Sacrosanctum Concilium*, set off the only and most important "reform"—strictly speaking—that the assembly of council fathers decided, that is, liturgical reform. Far from a reform confined to the aesthetics of the liturgy, *Sacrosanctum Concilium* had profound implications and affected both the ecclesiological debate (from October 1963 on) and Vatican II as such in its basic theological assumptions (such as *ressourcement*, the Church as the people of God, ecumenism) and in its institutional options alike (the creation of national bishops' conferences in every country).

The impact of the mass media on Vatican II was certainly much greater than on any other council of the Church, but also in comparison with any other religious event. The council's geographical setting in Rome (the capital of Catholicism), the "quasi-parliamentarian" mechanism in the *aula* on the floor of St. Peter's (the relationship between a majority and a minority; the system of plenary assemblies, commissions, and subcommissions; the amendments on the proposed texts; the lobbying outside the *aula*), the long duration of the event (seven years from its announcement in January 1959 to its conclusion in December 1965, with four very intense sessions in the autumn seasons between 1962 and 1965)—all of this provided the press, the radio, and the new media of television with a not-to-be-missed event of change within an institution, the Catholic Church, which had always held immutability as a strength. Vatican II gave the media a new face for global Catholicism, but to a certain extent it is undeniable that the media coverage of Vatican II also had an impact on developing in the bishops and theologians convened in Rome a new sense of the global dimension of the Church in its trying to reunite Christians: "Vatican II expresses, relative to this development, an embryonic inversion of this tendency."[5]

But most of all, it was the theological milieu and preconciliar movements of renewal (the liturgical, biblical, and ecumenical movements, and the patristic revivals) that provided the council fathers with insights for the debates. And from the theological milieu came, immediately after the end of Vatican II, the first wave of studies on the council documents.

VATICAN II: ACKNOWLEDGED, RECEIVED, REFUSED (1965–80)

On December 8, 1965, the end of Vatican II meant the return of bishops and theologians from Rome to their local Churches, but it did not mean the conclusion of the debates or the end of the Roman Curia's attempt to control the final outcome of the council. Certainly the final texts of the council had been voted on, definitively approved, and solemnly promulgated by Pope Paul VI in order to be translated and spread in the Catholic Church. In 1564, not long after the end of the Council of Trent, Pope Pius IV established the Congregation of the Council to be in charge of interpreting the decrees of the council and forbade the publication of any glosses or commentaries on them. The conclusion of Vatican II did not entail such prohibition on commenting on the final texts; hence, there was no implication that the Holy See and Roman Curia held a strict monopoly on the interpretation of the council texts—even if "the council was held in the center, named for the center, operated to a large extent with the equipment of the center, and was destined to be interpreted and implemented by the center."[6] Thus it comes as no surprise that the first opportunity for theologians to debate the council's final documents was given by a series of commentaries on the texts, published for theologians, priests, seminarians, and religious men and women, and also for a broad readership eager to gain more familiarity with the texts of Vatican II.[7]

Of particular interest is that the most important of these commentaries came not from bishops who oversaw the drafting process but from theologians who acted during Vatican II as consultants (*periti*) in the official commissions, or as private theologians serving their bishops during the preparations for their interventions in *aula* and in the council commissions.

Some of the authors of these commentaries became the main characters of the debate about Vatican II from the 1970s on (Yves Congar, Henri de Lubac, Joseph Ratzinger, Edward Schillebeeckx), and we will examine their positions in the following chapters. What is important to note now is the eminently academic background of these commentators—theologians by profession and not always holders of ecclesiastical offices with direct pastoral duties. In the meantime, the bishops were active on another level of the debate on Vatican II, having committed themselves to initiatives for an ecclesial reception of Vatican II through a significant wave of diocesan and national synods (Austria 1968–71, Netherlands 1970, and Germany 1972–75) and the continental assemblies of bishops (for Latin America the CELAM convened in Medellin in 1968). Moreover, the theological landscape of the first year of the post–Vatican II period began with a fruitful season of ecumenical dialogues.

This kind of "separation of tasks" between theologians and bishops is a feature of the debate on Vatican II and a marker of post–Vatican II Catholicism, at least until the end of the pontificate of John Paul II. He acted as the last and only guarantee for Vatican II, with a sometimes rather "nominalistic" yet unequivocal intention to receive the legacy of the council. John Paul II revisited in a creative way some crucial teachings of Vatican II, such as ecumenism in his encyclical *Ut unum sint* (1995) and interreligious dialogue beginning with the World Day of Prayer in Assisi (1986) and continuing in his travels, especially in the Middle East. On the other hand, the role of the bishops and of the national bishops' conferences in the interpretation of Vatican II in the life of the Church was reduced under Paul VI and even more under John Paul II. But a more significant and clear change happened in April 2005 with the election of Benedict XVI, who, as cardinal prefect for the Congregation for the Doctrine of the Faith (1981–2005), had been a powerful interpreter of Vatican II and not a mere enforcer of John Paul II's doctrinal policies.

The main commentaries on the final documents of the council represented an attempt to cast light on the deeper meaning of the texts against the background of the history of the debate, and to elaborate hypotheses on the Catholic Church's path after Vatican II. In the very first years after the council, the ideological spectrum of Catholic theologians on Vatican II seemed to be unanimous in their enthusiastic acceptance of the final documents and their view of the novelty of Vatican II, for example, in ecclesiology, liturgy, biblical revival, ecumenism, religious freedom, and interreligious relations. The tensions between the "letter" and the "spirit" of Vatican II did not play much of a role at that time, and neither did the supposed tension between the hermeneutic of continuity with the whole Catholic tradition and the awareness of a discontinuity from the Catholicism of the past, especially of the "long" nineteenth century from Pius IX to Pius XII.

The ranks of theologians in the so-called "majority" accepted the council as a major turning point. Nevertheless, the nuances of "how to read" Vatican II—with such terms as *application, reception, interpretation*—revealed important differences. That kind of theological unanimity about Vatican II—arising from the "moral unanimity" Paul VI sought for the approval of the final documents—would not last. Toward the end of the council, the debate concerning the content and the role of the pastoral constitution *Gaudium et spes* revealed the division within twentieth-century theologians between the neo-Augustinians (Daniélou, de Lubac, Ratzinger, von Balthasar) and the neo-Thomists (Chenu, Congar, Rahner, Lonergan, Schillebeeckx).[8]

The founding of the progressive Dutch-based journal *Concilium* in 1964 represented the most notable attempt to spread the message of Vatican II by a group of scholars representing the vast majority at the council (Hans Küng, Yves Congar, Karl Rahner, Edward Schillebeeckx). By 1970 the group already had important defections (Henri de Lubac, Hans Urs von Balthasar, Joseph Ratzinger), signaling a rupture in the theologians' attitude toward the council. A new international review, *Communio*, was founded in 1972 by Joseph Ratzinger, Hans Urs von Balthasar, and Henri de Lubac as an attempt to offset *Concilium* and to "scan the turmoil and confusion of battling ideologies and the clash of philosophies of life at the present day."[9] Writers for *Communio* preferred to interpret Vatican II with what they called a hermeneutic of continuity, emphasizing the council's solidarity with the whole Catholic tradition and the previous councils and a more Augustinian approach to the issue of the relationship between the Church and the modern world.

Paul VI's encyclical on contraception, *Humanae vitae* (released in 1968, a politically intense year around the world), greatly impacted the Church, took its toll on the reception of Vatican II, and produced the first "revisions" of the council's interpretations, inaugurating less enthusiastic and more wary views of the council, and also a way of reading the council that had more to do with ideological standpoints than with the history of theology and Church history.

The controversies of the early seventies for the Catholic Church did not bring together again the theologians of Vatican II, but contributed to an increasing rift between interpretations. On June 29, 1972, Paul VI, preaching on the Feast of Saint Peter and Paul, said: "After the Council, we believed there would be a day of sunshine in the history of the Church. Instead there arrived a day of clouds, of tempest, of darkness, of questioning, of uncertainty."[10] In particular, Paul VI's final defeat in drafting *Lex Ecclesiae Fundamentalis* ("Fundamental Church Law"), which tried to canonize a narrow ecclesiological interpretation of Vatican II, made the Holy See more and more wary toward some implementations of the council. The debates between 1965 and the mid-1970s on the need for this "Fundamental Church Law" (a law that was never promulgated but was "recycled" in many parts of the 1983 Code of Canon Law) showed the variety of interpretations of Vatican II present inside the Roman Curia and within the former "progressive" majority at the council.

The former "conservative" minority at the council proved more coherent in its fight against Vatican II. The small sect created by Archbishop Marcel Lefebvre in 1970—the Society of St.

Pius X—represented quite effectively the awkward (to say the least) features of a contemporary Catholicism that deliberately rejected Vatican II and attached itself to a premodern theological culture and antidemocratic political worldview.[11] The excommunication of Archbishop Lefebvre in 1976 did not have significant effects on the debate, but at the beginning of 2009, Benedict XVI's lifting of the excommunications of the four bishops ordained by Lefebvre in 1988 cast significant light on a veiled yet very active rift within European and North American Catholicism concerning the role of Vatican II.

Besides the very European Lefebvrian phenomenon, the debate on Vatican II in the mid-seventies gave rise to calls for a "Vatican Council III"—for the first time in a long series of recurrent yet short-lived appeals.[12] John Paul II's election in 1978 unleashed a new impulse for the reception of Vatican II by a bishop of Rome who, as bishop of Krakow, had been very active in the commission for the drafting of the pastoral constitution *Gaudium et spes,* and later as the author of a bulky commentary on the council.[13]

VATICAN II:
CELEBRATED AND ENFORCED (1980–90)

In the 1980s and 1990s, the debate on Vatican II focused less on the contributions from academia and began to become more influenced by the doctrinal policy of the Holy See, especially by Pope John Paul II and by Cardinal Joseph Ratzinger, Prefect of the Congregation for the Doctrine of the Faith (appointed in 1981). Both first-rank participants at Vatican II—the first a prominent bishop from Poland (the most Catholic country in the Soviet-controlled Eastern-European bloc) and the second a theological counselor of Cardinal

Frings of Cologne (one of the most important German bishops and a courageous critic of the Roman Curia during the debates on the floor of St. Peter)—they shaped a complex and sometimes contradictory Vatican policy toward the heritage of the council and its role for contemporary Catholicism.

After the theological interpretation of Vatican II that took place in the recodification of canon law, which led to the Code of 1983,[14] John Paul II convened an extraordinary assembly of the Synod of Bishops in 1985 on the twentieth anniversary of the end of the council to overcome polarization and bring about greater consensus. The conclusions of the synod provided the debate with some guidelines for the interpretation of the council, without questioning the riches of Vatican II, nor its key role for the future of the Catholic Church. In its report of its findings, the synod affirmed that

> the Council is a legitimate and valid expression and interpretation of the deposit of faith as it is found in Sacred Scripture and in the living tradition of the Church. Therefore we are determined to progress further along the path indicated to us by the Council.... [However, the synod did recognize] deficiencies and difficulties in the acceptance of the Council. In truth, there certainly have also been shadows in the post-council period, in part due to an incomplete understanding and application of the Council, in part to other causes. However, in no way can it be affirmed that everything which took place after the Council was caused by the Council.[15]

Concerning the issue of how to interpret Vatican II, the synod was resolute in explaining that "it is not licit to separate the pastoral character from the doctrinal vigor of the documents. In the same way, it is not legitimate to separate the spirit and the letter of the Council."[16] As for the relationships between these documents, the synod did not establish a clear hierarchy:

> The theological interpretation of the conciliar doctrine must show attention to all the documents, in themselves and in their close inter-relationship, in such a way that the integral meaning of the Council's affirmations—often very complex—might be understood and expressed. [Nevertheless,] special attention must be paid to the four major Constitutions of the Council, which contain the interpretative key for the other Decrees and Declarations.[17]

As for the continuity-discontinuity issue, the synod did not take a position for or against theological or historiographical "schools," but reaffirmed the complex relationship between tradition and transition in Catholic theology,[18] saying that "the Council must be understood in continuity with the great tradition of the Church, and at the same time we must receive light from the Council's own doctrine for today's Church and the men of our time. The Church is one and the same throughout all the councils."[19]

John Paul II's complex and sometimes contradictory orientation toward Vatican II, his decision to convene the synod of 1985, and the overall result of the synod for the state of the debate on Vatican II were somehow overshadowed by *The Ratzinger Report*, a book-length interview with him on the state of the church, timed to be published for the opening of the synod. *The Ratzinger Report* was aimed at exerting pressure on the bishops and on public opinion in order to make a case for rethinking the approach to Vatican II, and to point out the responsibility of the council in the crisis of post–Vatican II Catholicism.[20] Despite this, the synod provided theologians and historians with the opportunity to reflect on the reception of Vatican II twenty years after its conclusion. The publication of important collections of studies between 1985 and 1987 showed an obvious plurality of opinions and some differences between bishops and scholars, but not necessarily an unyielding tension and opposition between different hermeneutics of Vatican II.[21]

At the same time, the doctrinal policy of the Holy See toward some key issues of Vatican II, such as ecclesiology, began unfolding from the mid-1980s on, both through the Congregation for the Doctrine of the Faith and the International Theological Commission of the Holy See. The former issued a new profession of faith on March 1, 1989, for those who were called to exercise an office in the name of the Church (such as vicars general, episcopal vicars, rectors of a seminary, professors of theology and philosophy in seminaries and Catholic universities, and superiors in clerical religious institutes and societies of apostolic life). In addition, the Congregation for the Doctrine of the Faith also issued a letter to the bishops about the "ecclesiology of communion" (*Communionis notio*, May 28, 1992), as well as the "Declaration on the Unicity and Salvific Universality of Jesus Christ and the Church" about the relationship between Christ, the Church, and the non-Christian religions (*Dominus Iesus*, August 6, 2000). These marked two other important steps in the Roman reception of Vatican II. From the standpoint of the post–Vatican II governance of the Catholic Church, John Paul II's own apostolic constitution *Apostolos suos* (May 21, 1998) on the status and authority of episcopal conferences reinforced one of the basic assumptions of the International Theological Commission chaired by Cardinal Ratzinger, that is, the need to scale back some aspects of the post–Vatican II decentralization and empowerment of national bishops' conferences. It seemed that power was being reclaimed by the Church's head in Rome at the expense of the Church's body throughout the world.

VATICAN II: HISTORICIZED (1990–2000)

Notwithstanding the pressure of John Paul II's Vatican doctrinal policy on Catholic theologians, the most important wave of studies and research on Vatican II began in the late 1980s and early 1990s. In an international conference at the Centre Sèvres in Paris in December 1988, Giuseppe Alberigo started the enterprise that had its conclusion in 2001 with the five-volume *History of Vatican II*, subsequently published in seven languages.[22] Employing as a point of departure the first sources edited by Monsignor Vincenzo Carbone in the *Acta et Documenta* and *Acta Synodalia*,[23] as well as the first commentaries,[24] historical-critical studies of the texts,[25] journalistic accounts, personal memoirs, and sociological approaches to the event of Vatican II[26]—Alberigo headed an international network of scholars (theologians and historians from Europe, North America, and Latin America all working together) who took the first steps toward a comprehensive history of Vatican II. They aimed not at a new series of commentaries on the final documents, but at a scholarly reconstruction of the council as a historical event in a multivolume work that was parallel yet independent from some important syntheses[27] and proceedings of international conferences on Vatican II that took place after the Extraordinary Synod of 1985.[28]

The *History of Vatican II* represented a major scholarly and historiographical exploration of the debate on Vatican II. On one side, the undertaking, coordinated by Giuseppe Alberigo and the John XXIII Foundation for Religious Studies in

Bologna, called for a major effort in searching for undiscovered and unused archives of primary sources all over the world and in gaining access to the official sources (unpublished sources such as the acts of the preparatory phase, acts of the council commissions and committees, and reports and letters between the council's various bodies) that the Holy See held in the archive of Vatican II.[29] On the other side, the international and multidisciplinary character of the team provided the debate on Vatican II with many new questions, new issues and places for comparing perspectives, new results and paths of research.[30] The main hermeneutical principles that guided Alberigo in the enterprise were the idea of the council as an "event," John XXIII's intention in announcing the council, the pastoral nature of the council, *aggiornamento* as the main goal of the council, and the importance of compromise in understanding the council's final documents.[31]

The five-volume *History of Vatican II* was surrounded and followed by many other volumes produced and published by the same international team, focusing on individual constitutions and decrees and on specific issues debated at the council.[32] But the most important result was the spreading and the enlivening of the international debate on Vatican II in Latin America,[33] Europe,[34] America,[35] and all over the world,[36] in journals and reviews, and among theologians, historians, and lay women and men.

One of the earliest collections of commentaries on the final documents of Vatican II appeared shortly after the council: the three-volume *Zweite Vatikanische Konzil, Dokumente und Kommentare*, published in the series *Lexicon für Theologie und Kirche* between 1966 and 1968.[37] After Alberigo's work, theologian Peter Hünermann from Tübingen launched his own major project of commentaries, which was aimed at replacing the older three-volume set. In contrast with Alberigo's five-volume

History of Vatican II, Hünermann's five-volume *Kommentar zum Zweiten Vatikanischen Konzil* was a project entirely funded by and produced in the German-speaking world,[38] but meant to provide the international theological community with a significant contribution on the council forty years after its end.

TOWARD A NEW FIGHT OVER VATICAN II?

The fortieth anniversary of the conclusion of Vatican II in 2005 did not have any significant impact on the theological debate surrounding the council. Rather, the year was marked by the death of John Paul II, the conclave, and the election of Benedict XVI. But the death of John Paul II—the last bishop-participant at the council to be elected bishop of Rome—and the election of Benedict XVI constituted undoubtedly two important elements in the broad theological and ecclesiastical landscape of the debate on Vatican II in the last few years.

The change of pontificate also nourished the journalistic and political dispute about Vatican II's history and legacy, and not only the historiographical and theological debate. Since elected in April 2005, during the fortieth anniversary of the end of Vatican II, Benedict XVI has issued teachings that have increasingly renewed both ecclesiastical and public scrutiny on the council, and that have been bound up with the question about the legacy of the Vatican II–era in the vitality of the contemporary Catholic Church and its impact on the Western world.

After his address to the Roman Curia in December 2005, the Congregation for the Doctrine of the Faith released the document "Responses to Some Questions Regarding Certain Aspects of the Doctrine on the Church" (June 29, 2007) on the ecclesiology and interpretation of *"subsistit in"* (*Lumen gentium*

17

8), which contributed to the feeling of a new age. Benedict's teachings have reignited a debate about the long taken-for-granted role of Vatican II in the Catholic Church, leaving the impression of a Roman "attitude review" (if not "policy review") toward the council.[39]

His 2007 *motu proprio* on liturgy *Summorum Pontificum*, which allowed for greater use of the Latin Tridentine Mass, and his 2009 lifting of the excommunications of the four bishops ordained by Marcel Lefebvre, have focused a new kind of attention on the council and created a situation that is leading to a new understanding of its significance. The debate on the meaning of the council has entered a new stage. Pope Benedict's attempt to reabsorb this schism has revealed that Vatican II represents for the Catholic Church of the twenty-first century more than a compass for its future path, which is what John Paul II had hoped for in his encyclical *Novo millennio ineunte* (2001). Vatican II seems to have been received much more deeply beyond the borders of Catholicism, especially the *ad extra* statements of the council (on ecumenism, relationship with the Jews, religious freedom, and the Church and the modern world), whereas within the Catholic Church the debate on the interpretation of the core issues of Vatican II (especially the relationship between tradition, *ressourcement*, and *aggiornamento*) seems to be far from over.

In any case, the polemics and the reignited debate have proved somewhat useful as they have sparked a new interest in the hermeneutics of Vatican II, echoing a rooted argument about the hermeneutics of the council in its final "documents" versus in its "spirit," and making room for new studies focusing on what happened at Vatican II.[40]

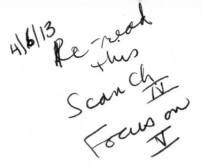

2

QUESTIONING THE LEGITIMACY OF VATICAN II

OPPOSITE EXTREMISMS

It has become common to affirm that the first years of the history of the reception of Vatican II were marked by exuberance and were soon followed by a sense of disappointment among those who were exuberant. This disappointment, presumably because of the slowness and indecision in the reforms intended to implement Vatican II in the life of the Church, has somehow come to define the main sentiments of many Vatican II theologians toward the council. The characterization has become so effective that Vatican II itself has sometimes been labeled, by liberal Catholics especially, a disappointment—far from the intentions of the theologians of the council. The sentiment has become a standard attitude in some areas of post–Vatican II Catholic theology, which took the council for granted, but, in the end, also regarded it a disappointment for breaking some of its promises.

Meanwhile, in recent years, traditionalist Catholics—that is, from the extremes of "sedevacantists" (who claim the Papal See has been vacant since the death of either Pius XII in 1958 or John XXIII in 1963) to the more moderate advocates of the Latin Mass—have grown much more vocal in denouncing the council as synonymous with disaster and chaos in the Church. Their negative view of the results of the liturgical reform could be applied uniformly to all of the major developments of Vatican II (ecclesiology, ecumenism, religious freedom, and the Church and the modern world) without altering their level of outrage.

Now Vatican II appears left out on a limb, especially when one considers that the generation of bishops and theologians who took part in Vatican II has faded from the scene, and the youngest generation of Catholics does not seem interested in understanding the message that Vatican II might bring to the future of the Church. But this way of reading the debate according to opposite extremisms is surely misleading if we consider the different theological and cultural roots of the interpreters of Vatican II. These go much deeper than "exuberance" and "disappointment."

The first pair of opposite viewpoints to consider regarding the debate on Vatican II—from a chronological as well as a logical point of view—concern the very legitimacy of the council and the acceptance of its teachings and effect in the Church. Conservative Catholics present as self-evident the assumption that the "crisis" in the Catholic Church was caused by a vanguard of radical Vatican II theologians willing to go beyond the council in order to prepare the ultimate rupture with the tradition of the Church through a call for "Vatican III." In truth, we can see that, in the fifty-year history of the debate on Vatican II, the real challenge to the legitimacy of the council came not from the ranks of the theologians who made it possible, but from a small fringe within the broader "council minority." This fringe contested not the effects of the council's reception but the very existence of Vatican II as a legitimate council in the tradition of the Church.

VATICAN II: A REFORM COUNCIL

In the first decade following the conclusion of the council in 1965, something was happening: in this period, "numerous books and articles appeared with titles indicating that something more than *reform* was underway,"[1] and in the 1970 congress held by the journal *Concilium* in Bruxelles, the watchword for the future was "beyond the council."[2] During this same period, however, the vast majority of bishops and Catholic theologians was still very much engaged in commenting on and applying the texts of Vatican II. This majority, composed of representatives of a "reformist" reception of the council documents, did not show the "revolutionary" attitude for which they were blamed by the small traditionalist minority, and for which they are now blamed by neo-traditionalist Catholic movements.

Far from radical in their interpretation of Vatican II in the first decade after the council, some of the most prominent bishops and theologians active in the reception of Vatican II called for a reform of the Church in accordance with the council documents. At the forefront of the reformers' minds were the completion of the liturgical reform, the implementation of collegiality in light of the new ecclesiology, the limitation of juridicism in the Church, the reform of the Roman Curia, the opening to the modern world, and the deepening of ecumenical dialogue.

As at the Council of Trent four centuries before, the first reformers were the bishops of Vatican II, the real driving force of the council. Appointed by Pius XI and Pius XII, and tempered by World War II and the Cold War, the bishops of Vatican II surely did not fear the challenge of implementing the council in their dioceses and in the universal Church, nor did they fear debating with Paul VI on how to apply some of the most delicate aspects of the council. In his interview in

Informations Catholiques Internationales in 1969, Cardinal Leo Jozef Suenens indicated the need for real collegiality in the Church and underlined the shortcomings of the new Synod of Bishops.[3] Like Suenens, Catholic bishops around the world, in their dioceses and in national bishops' conferences, worked on the reception of the council and never questioned the need to start from its documents in order to understand the spirit of the council and make it a tradition of the Church.

Yves Congar presents well the attitude of the theologians of Vatican II together with the bishops, and he is probably the most important theologian to look at the theological background and drafting of the council documents. In 1975, on the occasion of the tenth anniversary of the conclusion of the council, Congar affirmed two factors as important in the reception of Vatican II: "It is necessary (1) to have an historical sensibility and (2) [to] reckon with time, having the sense for the delay needed to understand, develop, apply, and mature things. It is necessary to give ourselves the time to digest Vatican II—a Vatican III or a Jerusalem II? Not so quickly!"[4]

Other theologians and historians profoundly engaged in the council debates during and after Vatican II offered a similar awareness at an international conference on "preparing for Vatican III" held at the University of Notre Dame in 1977. In his letter of invitation, the president of Notre Dame, Father Theodore M. Hesburgh, CSC, pointed out that the purpose of the conference was simply to see what scholarly research still needed to be accomplished in order to understand Vatican II: "The meeting is not designed to be a call for 'Vatican III'—a title intended to be symbolic—but rather to block out the scholarly research in theology and in the social sciences which needs to be done before the Church can come to its next critical turning point."[5]

The historians and theologians who spoke at Notre Dame represented the mainstream of Vatican II Catholicism and offered a courageous but realistic path for the future of the Church by drawing inspiration from the council. The Swiss theologian Hans Küng (a professor in Tübingen, Germany, at the time) did not seem as disappointed with the accomplishments of the reception of Vatican II in the first decade after 1965 as he later became: "The Catholic public today is in danger of forgetting the theological and practical successes of the past decade. These must be brought back into public awareness. In this way, those responsible for decision making in the church can be confronted once again with the state of theological research and of ecumenical practice."[6] The Italian historian Giuseppe Alberigo (the head of the Bologna school) expressed his perplexity regarding the need for and the viability of a "Vatican III": "Were the Catholic Church to celebrate a new general council, one can legitimately fear that it would constitute an occasion of regression rather than development, to the extent that it would almost inevitably stress those aspects specific to Catholicism, with the result of widening the distance and increasing the misunderstanding relative to the other traditions."[7]

The fidelity of mainstream Catholic theology to Vatican II meant rather undramatic work for university and seminary teachers who from 1966 onward transformed their courses on sacramental theology, on ecclesiology, and on anthropology. But that did not prevent difficulties in the process of the reception of the council's documents and in the philosophical, theological, and political challenges lying beneath the letter of the constitutions, decrees, and declarations of Vatican II. Also, there were rifts and tensions in the ranks of the leaders of the council. Paul VI's encyclical *Humanae vitae* (1968), Jacques Maritain's book *Le Paysan de la Garonne*,[8] the unprecedented removal from office of one of the leaders of Vatican II

(Cardinal Giacomo Lercaro, archbishop of Bologna), and the disappointments regarding the implementation of the newly created Synod of Bishops, together represented major moments in the council's difficult reception. However, they also witnessed the vitality of the Catholic Church as it debated how to interpret Vatican II, taking for granted both the need to accept and interpret its documents.

THE TRADITIONALISTS: OPPOSITION AND REJECTION OF THE COUNCIL

In opposition to the moderate and reformist attitude embodied by Paul VI, the questioning of the legitimacy of Vatican II created the first real discontinuity in the reception of a general council in the second millennium. Although it may seem paradoxical, the main accusers of Vatican II as a "rupture" with the tradition of the Church were the same ones who produced a schism that did not concern the interpretation of the council documents but questioned the very legitimacy of Vatican II as a council in the tradition of the Church, its previous councils, and papal magisterium.

Even if the traditionalist movement became more and more radical in the late 1970s and in the 1980s, extreme opposition to the council did not wait a decade after the end of Vatican II to disavow it. Paul VI's incrementalist and reformist attitude and efforts to maintain the unity of the Church around the "moral unanimity" that approved the documents on the floor of St. Peter's Basilica could not appease the small fringe of bishops and theologians who had gathered after Vatican II at the request of the French archbishop Marcel Lefebvre. This kind of opposition, or negative reception of Vatican II, had already begun when the council was still far from its conclusion.

The coexistence of a majority vis-à-vis a minority of bishops constituted the core political and theological mechanics of Vatican II, at least during the debates and in the commissions of the council between 1962 and 1965.[9] The minority opposed the direction of the council documents in all the major issues: liturgical reform, biblical renewal, a "people of God" ecclesiology, reform of the Roman Curia, ecumenism, religious freedom, and the Church and the modern world.[10] The idea of change in the Church was the real enemy of the council's minority.

The debates led to practical unanimity in the bishops' votes approving the documents. Opposition to some core statements did not vanish, but part of the conservative minority was gradually convinced of the need for change in the Church, or were convinced by Paul VI of the need to have the council documents approved by the moral unanimity of the Vatican II bishops. A considerable number of bishops, among them some of the leaders of the conservative minority (such as Cardinal Giuseppe Siri and Cardinal Alfredo Ottaviani, the secretary of the Holy Office, whose episcopal motto was, significantly, *Semper idem*—"always the same"), continued fighting after Vatican II for their interpretation of the council. They viewed it as a dangerous and potentially catastrophic event for the Catholic Church, but did not immediately organize a breakaway or schismatic group. The great part of the conservative minority remained in a Church that was changing, largely because it was not changing as dramatically as they had feared.

However, in October 1964 during the third session, some members of the conservative minority joined a few leaders, spokespersons, and an informal group of about two hundred bishops from different countries—mostly Latin America, Italy, and Spain—called the Coetus Internationalis Patrum ("International Group of Fathers) and fundamentally contested the legitimacy of the council following its conclusion.[11] Their opposition to Vatican II was much more intense and could not be satisfied by the "pastoral diminution" of the council, a tool widely used to minimize Vatican II: labeling it a merely pastoral and not a dogmatic council was a way to demote the council's theological change of direction to a series of purely rhetorical concessions to the modern language. Therefore, a tiny group of ultraconservative bishops chose to go from being part of the opposition within Vatican II to constituting a complete rejection of Vatican II. Their position embodied the pillar of the internal dissent within the Catholic Church engaged in the reception of Vatican II.

To accomplish this, they needed a narrative of Vatican II that provided a necessary element in the creation of sectarian groups of any kind: a conspiracy. A sizable factor in the ideological mind-set of the rejection of Vatican II was the creation of the myth of a "northern European maneuvering," based on the fact that the largest and most influential group at the council consisted of fathers and experts from Germany, Austria, Switzerland, France, the Netherlands, and Belgium. Ralph Wiltgen's well-informed book *The Rhine Flows into the Tiber* has been used by advocates of the rejection of Vatican II, even though Wiltgen distanced himself from the mind-set of the conspiracy: "[The advocates] charge that the Council's sixteen documents have been vitiated, even invalidated by pressure groups. Apparently not everyone is aware that the formation of thought groups in Vatican II was as natural a process as it is in any other legislative assemblies."[12] Strangely enough, some of the leaders who rejected Vatican II came from that very part of Europe.

One theologian stood between the internal opposition to Vatican II and the Lefebvrian rejection of the council: Romano Amerio (1905–97), born in Lugano, Switzerland, but Italian by nationality. Amerio, an episcopal consultant to the central preparatory commission of Vatican II (1960–62) and an expert during the council for bishop Angelo Giuseppe Jelmini (apostolic administrator of Lugano), published a book in 1985 (the year of the special Synod of Bishops for the twentieth anniversary of Vatican II) that has become very popular in neo-traditionalist groups. In *Iota Unum: A Study of Change in the Catholic Church in the Twentieth Century*, Amerio provides an interpretation of Vatican II that brings him much closer to the rejection of Vatican II voiced by the Lefebvrian schism rather than to the neo-traditionalist wave of Catholicism that so often refers to him. In the first chapter, Amerio essentially equates the words *change* and *crisis*, opting to use *change* in the book's subtitle because the word better depicts the long duration of the epochal crisis in which twentieth-century Catholicism found itself, mostly due to the change precipitated by Vatican II. Examining the contents of Amerio's book proves that nothing escapes his assessment of Vatican II as the culmination of early twentieth-century Modernism and its corruption of every issue: sacraments, priesthood, catechetics, natural law and ethics, the Church and women, and eschatology.

Despite his decision to remain in the Catholic Church after Vatican II, and despite his recent adoption by some neo-traditionalist circles close to Rome, Amerio's criticism of the council does not stop with a catastrophist assessment of liturgical reform. The author blames Vatican II for having "outstripped the council that had been prepared" by the Roman Curia, and for having emphasized—like many others did—the ambiguous character of the conciliar texts, which made it possible that "the spirit of the council outstripped the council itself."[13]

Amerio's historical case for Vatican II as the main agent for radical discontinuity in the tradition of the Church, due to the continuity between Modernism and Vatican II teachings, renders his attack on the council much more extremist than others. In the epilogue of his book, "The Change in the Church as *Hairesis*," Amerio offers a clear-cut and straightforward definition of Vatican II as a heresy:

> While considering this loss of unity in doctrine we might remind ourselves of its depth and, above all, of its swiftness by referring to the false analyses and forecasts made about the Church's doctrinal unity around the time of the council. In his pastoral letter for Lent 1962, Cardinal Montini, the Archbishop of Milan, said that "today there are no errors in the Church, or scandals or deviations or abuses to correct" and when he had become Pope he said in his first encyclical *Ecclesiam Suam* in 1964 that: "At the present time it is no longer a matter of ridding the Church of this or that particular heresy or of certain specific disorders. Thanks be to God there are none in the Church." The precisely opposite kind of statements the same Pope Paul VI was making toward the end of his reign, proclaiming that there was a grave crisis in the Church, arouse questions concerning not only psychology, but also principles of interpretation and the nature of God's dealings with the world. But we are here concerned with emphasizing the loss of unity in doctrine. If it is not entirely true to say, as Cardinal Suenens has, that there are a goodly number of propositions that used to be taught in Rome before the council as definite truths, that the council itself proceeded to discard, it is nonetheless true to say that what used to be a single voice in matters of doctrine is now a host of discordant voices instead. This is the effect of a loss of

virtue of faith itself, rather than the result of a series of disagreements in detail. In that sense, what Paul VI said is true; there are no particular errors to condemn; what needs to be condemned is an error of principle, because the host of particular errors in question do not relate to some subordinate aspect of Christianity but flow from a distinct anti-principle which was identified and condemned by St. Pius X under the name of Modernism.[14]

The definition of Vatican II as the ultimate and final moment of early twentieth-century Modernism has almost become, at the beginning of the twenty-first century, common language in the neo-traditionalist movement within contemporary Catholicism.[15] But it should be noted that this view of Vatican II as the epitome of all the heresies attacking Catholicism today is a sign of the rejection of the council in its purest form, because it comes—like the Lefebvrians—from inside the Catholic Church.

THE LEFEBVRIAN SCHISM AND VATICAN II

The opposition to the council has several faces (groups, movements, currents of thought, periodicals), spread around the world but based in Europe, with some North and South American affiliations.[16] At one extreme of the spectrum of traditionalist attitudes toward Vatican II are the sedevacantists, who assume that Rome is in a *sede vacante* situation due to Paul VI's promulgation of the acts of a council opposed to tradition and therefore schismatic and heretical. They judge Vatican II to have departed from tradition and to have taught heresy. In their opinion, Paul VI ceased formally to be pope; his successors to the papacy, elected by cardinals he appointed, were invalidly elected, thus their decisions are not to be obeyed. The sedevacantists' astounding view of Vatican II is matched only by their irrelevance. On the other hand, opposition to the council is also present in associations that profess obedience to the pope and to the bishops, but that fight for a return to a pre–Vatican II Church. Daniele Menozzi describes this phenomenon: "Between these two extremes there is a broad gamut of tendencies that are in dialogue or, more often, disagreement with one another."[17]

The most famous group to denounce Vatican II as heretical is the Society of St. Pius X, founded in 1970 by Archbishop Marcel Lefebvre (1905–91). He declared his rejection of Vatican II and in 1988 subsequently incurred automatic excommunication (*excommunicatio latae sententiae*) for having consecrated four priests of his society as bishops.[18] Lefebvre, formerly archbishop of Dakar and superior general of the Congregation of the Holy Spirit, was intensely involved in the council from the very beginning. Appointed by John XXIII as a member of the central preparatory commission, Lefebvre saw that the Roman Curia's preparation for the council between 1959 and 1960 had been criticized and dismantled by the reaction of the bishops around the world before the council.[19] Lefebvre soon became a leader of the conservative minority at Vatican II and a very vocal opponent of the major reforms of the council, in particular, the liturgical reform, episcopal collegiality, religious freedom, and ecumenism. During Vatican II, the *Coetus Internationalis Patrum* and the conciliar minority succeeded in convincing Paul VI of the need to counterbalance the gains of the conciliar majority. This led to the declaration of Mary as "Mother of the Church" (November 21, 1964) and the *Nota explicativa praevia* (November 16, 1964), which offered an official and narrow interpretation of chapter 3 of *Lumen gentium* on episcopal collegiality.[20] In the end, however, Vatican II was a sound defeat for Lefebvre and for the archconservative group within the council minority.[21]

Lefebvre was one of the seventy council fathers—representing about 3 percent of the total—who voted against the "Declaration on Religious Liberty" (*Dignitatis humanae*) on December 7, 1965. It was no surprise that he became one of the most constant critics of Vatican II, especially after 1972. Lefebvre accused Vatican II and Paul VI of having moved away from the sound tradition of the Church and from the magisterium, and of having imposed new dogmas derived from modern culture: progress, evolution, change. The pastoral character of Vatican II was interpreted by Lefebvre as a self-defense of Vatican II, a council incapable of dealing with dogmas and intent on introducing liberal ideas into the Catholic Church. Lefebvre saw Vatican II as a council that was "changing our religion."[22]

Like many other reactionaries, Lefebvre saw a liberal-Protestant-Masonic conspiracy behind change and, therefore, behind Vatican II. He did not distinguish between the council texts and the spirit of Vatican II as he defined that spirit. He acknowledged that the final documents of Vatican II *were* the fruit of the spirit of the council, while noting that "the spirit that mastered the council and inspired so many ambiguous, equivocal, and frankly even erroneous texts is not the Holy Spirit, but the spirit of the modern world, a liberal spirit, of Teilhard [de Chardin], modernist."[23]

Some points from the council particularly interested Lefebvre: First, he was opposed to episcopal collegiality, which he had already labeled in October 1963 as "collectivism," and found it impossible to reconcile the new ecclesiology of Vatican II with an ecclesiology heavily marked by an ultramontanist and hierarchical mentality. Second, the "Declaration on Religious Freedom" constituted for Archbishop Lefebvre—who, as a missionary in Senegal, had been a challenger of Islam and of animism in Africa—a theological legalization of apostasy: "Religious liberty is the major aim of Liberalism. Liberals, Masons, and Protestants are fully aware that by this means [sic!] they can strike at the very heart of the Catholic Church."[24] Third, the liturgical reform introduced "Luther's Mass" into the Catholic Church and, for the sake of ecumenical irenicism, endangered the preservation of tradition and the correct understanding of the Eucharist as renewal of Christ's sacrifice. Nevertheless, the real issue for Lefebvre and for his followers was the relationship between tradition and Vatican II. The council enlarged the concepts of tradition and revelation, thus changing the Church's understanding of human history as a source for theology and magisterium. According to Lefebvre's idea of Church, Catholic theology was the unchangeable deposit of the faith translated in historical-ideological terms. Completely alien to his antihistorical approach was the notion that revelation could be revealed in the history of the people of God and that therefore history had to serve as a source of theological discourse.

The political dimension of the rejection of Vatican II is clear in Lefebvre's position, since it is certainly true for the anticonciliar position that the contemporary political climate often determines the view of the state of the Church. In particular, the view of Vatican II as "the French revolution in the Church" was fundamental in shaping Lefebvre's historical perception of the council, especially for a French bishop such as himself, faithful to the idea of a chain of "modern errors" (like the sixteenth-century Reformation followed by the Enlightenment, the French Revolution, liberalism, and socialism, and then culminating in twentieth-century communism). Lefebvre—who had expressed support in the 1940s for the "Catholic order" of the authoritarian French Vichy régime (which collaborated with Nazi Germany), for authoritarian governments and military dictatorships in the 1970s (in Spain, Portugal, Chile, and Argentina), and for the French far-right party the National Front in the 1980s—added Vatican II as the final link in this chain of "modern errors." In his *Open Letter to Confused Catholics* (1986), Lefebvre described this chain of events: "The parallel I have drawn between the crisis in the Church and the French Revolution is not simply a metaphorical one. The influence of the *philosophes* of the eighteenth century, and of the upheaval that they produced in the world, has continued down to our times. Those who injected that poison admit it themselves."[25]

The rejection of the new liturgy and the defense of, as Lefebvre described it in his book, the "Mass of all times" against the "Mass of our time" is the most well-known point of dissent between his group and Vatican II supporters. Lefebvre took seriously the strong relationship between the liturgical constitution and Vatican II as a whole, with the post-conciliar liturgical renewal being the first and indefeasible step toward the full implementation of the council. But the liturgical reform was only one element in Lefebvre's much broader challenge to Vatican II.[26] He stated that the "poisoners" of the council

> constituted a minority, but an active and organized minority, supported by a galaxy of modernist theologians amongst whom we find all the names who since then have laid down the law, names like Leclerc, Murphy, Congar, Rahner, Küng, Schillebeeckx, Besrel, Cardonnet, Chenu, etc. And we must remember the enormous output of printed matter by IDOC, the Dutch information center subsidised by the German and Dutch Bishops' Conferences. It created a sort of psychosis, a feeling that one must not disap-

point the expectations of the world which is hoping to see the Church come round to its views.[27]

According to Lefebvre, the pastoral character of the council was one of the main signs of its weakness. He perceived the new literary style of the council documents as a way to disguise their contents and their disruption of the Catholic tradition, saying in his *Open Letter to Confused Catholics*: "This was not through negligence or by chance. Those people knew what they were doing. All the other councils that have been held during the course of the centuries were dogmatic. All have combated errors. Now God knows what errors there are to be combated in our times! A dogmatic council would have filled a great need." Among the errors neglected by Vatican II, he continued, the most insidious enemy to his *Weltanschauung* was communism: "The most monstrous error ever to emerge from the mind of Satan...has official access to the Vatican. This refusal of this pastoral council to solemnly condemn it is enough in itself to cover it with shame before the whole history."[28] In attacking communism in staunch defense of the Catholic Church, Lefebvre was a late advocate of the political ideology of that faction of early twentieth-century Catholicism that in Europe had built its credentials of defender of civilization and natural law (obliterated by communists), as a bastion of anticommunist and philo-fascist sentiment. Despite the historical fact that the bishops from communist Europe beyond the Iron Curtain begged the council not to issue a condemnation of communism, for Lefebvre, Vatican II's refusal to solemnly condemn communist ideology was proof of the philo-communist ideology of many bishops and theologian leaders of the council.

Lefebvre defined himself as neither a heretic nor a schismatic, and in his harsh judgment of the modern Church, he associated Vatican II with Paul VI's "liberalism." He appealed to every Catholic to disobey in matters such as religious liberty and collegiality in the Church. His assessment of the state of the Church after Vatican II was inextricably connected with his firm attachment to a very narrow idea of pontifical magisterium that developed after the French Revolution and to the ultramontanist mind-set typical of nineteenth-century Catholicism. He identified the idea of Church teaching with the contents and forms of nineteenth-century papal magisterium, culminating in Pius X's encyclical *Pascendi Dominici Gregis* (1907), which condemned modernism and had brought about the most dramatic purge of theologians in the modern history of the Catholic Church.

For Lefebvre, Vatican II represented the decisive point in the development of Catholicism in the modern world, a path that went from Christian democracy to Christian socialism and concluded with "Christian atheism," in which "dialogue" had become the most dangerous attitude: "The adulterous union of the Church and the Revolution is cemented by 'dialogue.' Truth and error are incompatible; to dialogue with error is to put God and the devil on the same footing."[29] According to Lefebvre, Vatican II had become the work of the devil against the Church: "There is no more any Magisterium, no dogma, nor hierarchy; not Holy Scripture even, in the sense of an inspired and historically certain text. Christians are inspired directly by the Holy Spirit. The Church then collapses."[30]

DIFFERENT DESTINIES FOR VATICAN II'S FRINGE GROUPS

While Lefebvre employed a narrative of the council as allegedly inspired by Freemasons and infiltrated by Communists, at the opposite end of the ideological spectrum were the groups of "Christians for socialism" in Europe and in

Latin America that asserted that "Vatican II represented the high point in the Church's effort to adapt itself to the bourgeois form of society."[31] Intra-ecclesial reform and the detachment of the Church from politics were seen by the Christians for socialism as the most telling signs of Catholic appeasement to capitalist society and, therefore, a renunciation of support for the revolutionary struggle.

As it has become clear in the last two decades, the destinies of these two fringes in the theological-ideological spectrum regarding Vatican II could not have been more different. On one side, the Christians for socialism and their interpretation of Vatican II never became a real interpreting force of the council and soon faded in the 1970s after the cultural failure of the so-called *gauchisme catholique*, active in Italy and in France especially. Both as a political group and as a Catholic movement, it disappeared soon from the cultural landscape of Western Catholicism in the early 1980s.[32] On the other side, the influence of the council minority on Vatican II's interpretation has been persistent and effective in influencing the reception of the council, much more persistent than the council majority could have possibly expected. As John O'Malley described it, "On the final outcome of the council the minority left more than a set of fingerprints."[33]

During the fourth session of Vatican II, the Roman Curia, very sympathetic to the opposition to the change, underwent some reform under Paul VI (the internationalization of the curial staff and the creation of the Synod of Bishops). The reform of the Roman Curia thus left the hardliners of the extremist opposition to the council outside, making the Curia an integral part of the process of the reception-application of Vatican II.[34]

The role of the Roman Curia after the Council of Trent was perfectly consistent with the institutional architecture of the "executive branch" in the hand of the popes:[35] in 1564 Pius IV created the Sacred Congregation of the Council (*Congregatio pro executione et interpretatione concilii Tridentini*), which was in charge of the application of the decrees of the Council of Trent and of the interpretation of the canons of the council. But the decentralization and the emphasis on the local Churches in the ecclesiology of Vatican II were not applied to the institutional framework of the Holy See and the Roman Curia themselves. The continuity between the pre–Vatican II Curia and the structure of the post–Vatican II Curia has had an impact on the reception of the council and on the survival of the anticonciliar reactionaries: "No postconciliar commission was established that corresponded to the Doctrinal Commission of Vatican II. Doctrinal problems fell again directly under the jealously preserved competence of the Holy Office."[36] Even after the excommunication of Lefebvre, the cultural ties between some offices of the Roman Curia and the anti–Vatican II sentiment were far from over.

Paul VI's balancing of reform and of the continuity of the institutional tradition did not prevent the conservative hardliners from loudly denouncing the "heresy" of Vatican II.[37] Their media outreach has recently become more intense and effective, but their interpretation of Vatican II has not changed from the position of the "founding father" of the rejection of the council, Marcel Lefebvre. In the meantime, the Church moved on to a new stage in its reception of Vatican II.

VATICAN II: BEYOND ROME

VATICAN II AS THE BEGINNING

In the foreword to his book *After the Council* (1968), the Lutheran theologian Edmund Schlink (1903–84), an ecumenical observer at Vatican II, quoted Karl Rahner's definition of the council as "the beginning of the beginning" of the *aggiornamento*.[1] This view of Vatican II as "the beginning" has been shared not only by non-Catholic theologians trying to grasp the significance of the council for their churches and for their theological traditions, but also by many Catholic theologians engaged in the debate about Catholicism and decolonization, Catholic theology and human liberation, and feminist theology and intercultural theology, from the very beginning of the theological reception of Vatican II.

The idea of Vatican II as the beginning of a new path for Catholic theology has been a pillar of conciliar hermeneutics from the very start of the debate until at least the 1990s, when the focus of the discussion shifted from the possible theological orientations of this beginning, to the study of the basis of the *event* of the beginning that was Vatican II. But this fundamental assumption about the pivotal role of Vatican II and its continuity/discontinuity with the past (without, however, making the pre–Vatican II era an "unusable past" for Catholic theology) is still the starting point for an understanding of the cultural, pastoral, and political issues underlying the theological debate. The ecumenical appraisal of Vatican II also contributed to forming the global perception of the council as being significant as well for Christians outside the Catholic Church.

VATICAN II AND ITS ECUMENICAL APPRAISAL

From the very beginning—during the council and after the council—the ecumenical observers took part in the debate on Vatican II. Before the commencement of Vatican II, the Vatican had consulted the World Council of Churches in Geneva through the Pontifical Secretariat for Promoting Christian Unity (created by John XXIII in 1960) and subsequently sent an official invitation to the non-Catholic Churches who accepted, with a few exceptions, the offer to go to Rome and "observe" the council in the making. There were forty official observers sent by their churches in the first session of Vatican II in 1962 (non-Chalcedonian Churches of the Middle East, Lutherans, Reformed, Anglicans, Disciples of Christ, Congregationalists, Quakers).[2] The late arrival of the Orthodox observers at Vatican II helped the total numbers of the ecumenical presence at the council rise to 103 in the last session in 1965, but many more non-Catholic observers and guests took part in Vatican II, bringing the total at the end of the council to more than 180.[3]

The ecumenical observers attended the four periods from 1962 to 1965 and had good seats in the Basilica of St. Peter for the debates. They took part at Vatican II officially as "observers" sent by their churches, but some of them worked as nonofficial theological advisors for the drafting of some conciliar documents particularly sensitive to ecumenical issues (especially about the Bible and revelation, ecclesiology, religious freedom, and ecumenism). The Lutheran theologian André Birmelè observes: "Their presence contributed undeniably to the new ecumenical awareness of the Catholic Church at Vatican II and influenced the work of the council."[4] Their contribution had a notable impact on the ecumenical character of the *corpus* of the final documents of Vatican II. In turn, the effect also worked in the other direction: as the council had its influence on the observers, they then influenced the general appreciation of the council as significant for all Christians.

Many ecumenical observers shared the same view of Vatican II as a moment of renewal for the Catholic Church—both in continuity and in discontinuity with the past—not through a reaffirmation of the unchangeable nature of its dogmatic definitions, but through the faithfulness to the substance of the faith. In the eyes of the ecumenical observers, at Vatican II the Catholic Church became more prepared to listen to the needs of the contemporary human being, and used a new language that showed an evolution in Catholicism without renouncing its original characteristics in terms of ecclesiology, sacraments, and the preservation of the deposit of faith.[5]

The liturgical reform was welcomed by ecumenical observers such as Karl Barth (1886–1968) and even by the Orthodox theologian Olivier Clément (1921–2009), who saw in the reform an example for the Orthodox liturgy, in which the faithful assume a mere passive role.[6] But from a theological point of view, what played remarkably well with ecumenical observers was the idea developed by Vatican II in the Decree on Ecumenism (*Unitatis redintegratio*) of a "hierarchy of truths."[7] The Decree said:

The Catholic faith must be explained more profoundly and precisely, in such a way and in such terms as our separated brethren can also really understand.

Moreover, in ecumenical dialogue, Catholic theologians standing fast by the teaching of the Church and investigating the divine mysteries with the separated brethren must proceed with love for the truth, with charity, and with humility. When comparing doctrines with one another, they should remember that in Catholic doctrine there exists a "hierarchy" of truths, since they vary in their relation to the fundamental Christian faith. Thus the way will be opened by which through fraternal rivalry all will be stirred to a deeper understanding and a clearer presentation of the unfathomable riches of Christ. (*Unitatis redintegratio* 11)

Each non-Catholic theologian who observed the council and analyzed the final documents developed his own interpretation of Vatican II. Even before the beginning of the council, the Danish Lutheran theologian Kristen E. Skydsgaard (1902–90) had expressed his expectations of the council on some issues close to the Catholic-Lutheran divide, especially concerning the relationship between Word and Church. Skydsgaard was curious about the "language" of the council: "The question is: *What* will be said, and *how* will it be said? Language and understanding belong together, but often they do not coincide at all. We all live under the curse of Babel."[8]

The representatives of the Anglican Church approached Vatican II with a history of dialogue and conversations with the Roman Catholic Church, even if the relationship between the two remained ambiguous in England because of the dominant attitude among Catholic bishops to "win back" England for the Catholic Church. The chief Anglican observer at the Second Vatican Council from 1962 to 1965 was the bishop of Ripon, John Moorman (1905–89), who was most active (also thanks to his fluency in Italian) in making a contribution at Vatican II on the basis of the close relationship between the theological traditions of the two Churches. During Vatican II, Moorman stated that it was important to mark the Anglican presence at the council: "The Anglicans must make their own contribution rather than allow the Methodists, Congregationalists and others to speak on behalf of them."[9] Moorman explained, both at Vatican II and from the very beginning of the postconciliar period, that the council had fundamentally changed the relations between the Catholic Church and the other Churches:

> The result of the Council has been to alter the whole ecumenical pattern and to carry the ecumenical discussion into a new field....Rome has, at last, begun to interest herself in the problem of unity, and things can never be the same again....The ecumenical problem in 1966 is quite different from what it was in 1961. A new pattern has emerged as a result of the Council, and much of the thought and language which was valid five years ago is now obsolete.[10]

This view of Vatican II as a truly ecumenical council was witnessed by the fact that Moorman, an expert on Saint Francis of Assisi and the history of the Franciscans, became the chairman of the Anglican commission in 1967, which led to the Anglican-Roman Catholic International Commission (ARCIC), of which Moorman remained a member until 1981.

Vatican II: Beyond Rome

The German Lutheran theologian Edmund Schlink was, like Moorman, engaged in the council as an "observer," but Schlink had a more comprehensive view of the significance of Vatican II as the founder of the Ecumenical Institute at the University of Heidelberg in 1946 (the first ecumenical institute in a German university), *and* in light of his role in the World Council of Churches. Schlink, who significantly helped shape the ecumenical movement's reading of Vatican II, witnessed the making of Vatican II and reported regularly to the World Council of Churches about the unfolding of the council and the critical advancement made by Catholic theology during it, especially regarding the interpretation of Scripture in the Church.[11] He prophetically saw in Vatican II not just the *corpus* of the final documents, but that Vatican II was an "event" destined to produce more progress in the years to come:

> The Council is more than its resolutions. One who knows only the resolutions of the Council has not yet grasped the conciliar event as a whole. The Council produced the breakthrough of a dynamic that is more comprehensive and more progressive than is expressed in the conciliar resolutions....Without doubt the conciliar decisions are correctly interpreted only if they are interpreted against the background of the whole conciliar event.[12]

The very experience of Schlink as an ecumenical observer at Vatican II made him acutely aware of the intense dynamics of the debate at the council and of the dialectic between "conservative forces" and "progressive forces":

> While the "conservatives" believe they have salvaged for the future many an item about which they had

been anxious, many of the "progressives" view such disagreements and tensions as the dialectic of an historical progress which the Council has made possible. Indeed, many see precisely these unresolved aspects as giving expression to the Council's dynamics which point to the future. Hence these tensions must be evaluated not only as a weakness inhering in the resolutions of the Council, but also as symptoms of the awakening of the Roman Church.[13]

Schlink saw the tensions within Vatican II as signs of the awakening of the Roman Church and as the *incipit*, the "beginning," of a movement that initiated with the council and moved toward a different engagement of modern Catholicism with the other Churches and with the modern world:

> Nevertheless, to speak only of individual reforms achieved by the Council would be to underestimate the Council. There came into being a movement of renewal which reaches further than the individual resolutions—a movement which has taken hold of many hearts in the Roman Church so that they yearn to serve God and their fellow men with greater faithfulness, devotion, openness, and love.[14]

Schlink knew that the postconciliar period for the Catholic Church would not be easy, but at the same time he expressed the deep conviction that Vatican II had been an ecumenical event in the sense that it had altered the theological *status quo* not only for the Catholic Church but also for non-Roman Churches:

> Vatican II will be taken seriously only when non-Roman Churches view it as a question addressed to themselves. Some of the questions which arise specif-

ically for the Evangelical Church have been mentioned. It will be up to the representatives of other churches to express their ways in which the Council represents a question addressed to their churches. It should not be doubted that the Council poses questions for them also.[15]

The Lutheran theologian Oscar Cullmann (1902–99), one of the most prominent ecumenical observers at Vatican II, pointed out the main theological feature of the ecumenical potential of Vatican II, that is, the rediscovery of Scripture and of the biblical hermeneutics as essential for theological work, which made possible the return of the Church to its biblical origins. On the hermeneutics of the council, Cullmann shared with other observers a similar view of the relationship between Vatican II as an event and the final documents of the council. Author of *Christ and Time* and the person responsible for the establishment of dialogue between Catholics and Lutherans, Cullmann was also well aware that Vatican II was more than its final documents, given the importance of the "impulses" activated by Vatican II: "More than in any other council here it was about the whole event of the council, whose impulses were active in the future not less than the final texts."[16] Cullmann noted: "From the beginning to the end of Vatican II the progressive majority was much more represented than the conservatives."[17] At the same time, he rejected both the "revolutionary" and the "continuist" interpretations of Vatican II. He saw a fundamental doctrinal continuity of the theological tradition of the Catholic Church without denying the renewal taking place in the conciliar Church: "Both [the revolutionary and the continuist] answers are wrong. From an historical point of view, Vatican II managed to renew Catholicism, as it was impossible before in its long history, without changing the fundamentals of the Catholic Church (some of which we as Protestants reject)."[18]

The Swiss Reformed theologian Karl Barth was no less interested in the Second Vatican Council. The Pontifical Secretariat for Promoting Christian Unity invited him as an observer, but he could not take part for health reasons. Barth visited Rome one year after the council's conclusion to gather information about it, and during the winter semester of 1966 to '67 he taught a seminar at the University of Basel on the constitution *Dei Verbum*.[19] Barth saw Vatican II as a fundamental moment in the life of the Churches: "Both the convocation and the previous course of the Council are symptomatic of a certain landslide that is taking place in the Roman Church, a *spiritual* movement taking place there, with whose possibility no one had reckoned fifty years ago."[20] Barth still had issues with Catholic doctrine on Mariology and papal infallibility, but he saw the Council as the beginning of a movement:

> We should direct our attention far more to what is beginning to appear as a movement of renewal *within* the Roman Church, to what in fact has already been partially set in motion, rather than to the possibilities of a loyal correspondence between us and its representatives....We *non-Roman* Christians are in a special way the ones who are *questioned*. Certainly, we are not asked whether we could, should, or would wish to become "Catholic," but we are asked whether, in view of the spiritual motion that is taking place there, something has been set in motion—or not set in motion!—on *our* side, in the rooms of *our* church.[21]

Barth went prophetically as far as fearing a possible exchange of roles, in the near future, between a more "evangelical" Catholic Church and the Protestant world: "Must not the council give us the occasion to sweep away the dust before the door of our own Church with a careful but nevertheless mighty broom?"[22]

The American Lutheran theologian George Lindbeck (1923–), one of the Lutheran observers at the council and, from 1968 to 1987, member of the Joint Commission between the Vatican and Lutheran World Federation—was less optimistic about the future of ecumenism, but no less convinced of the epoch-making character of Vatican II. Already during Vatican II Lindbeck had expressed his concerns about the consequences of the ecumenical reorientation of the Roman Church for Protestants:

> Many people...fear that if the churches of a given confessional or denominational family increasingly act together in ecumenical matters, this will lead to an unfortunate fragmentation of the ecumenical movement, a decrease in the role of the WCC, and a tendency for the dialogue to polarize around Rome. These are real dangers.[23]

Nevertheless, Lindbeck was convinced of the need for a historically sensitive hermeneutics of Vatican II. Already in 1970, he criticized some literalist approaches to interpreting the council:

> Many skeptical commentators strive to be "soberly realistic" about the extent of the present Catholic renewal. They interpret the Council legalistically and non-situationally in a kind of hermeneutical vacuum, sealed off from consideration of the concrete

situation in which it took place. In order to avoid overoptimism, they refuse to be impressed by any except the most unequivocal changes. They resolve all ambiguities in favor of interpretations which are most in continuity with rigid versions of Tridentine and Vatican I conservatism.[24]

Twenty years after his report was sent to the World Council of Churches, Lindbeck confirmed his view of Vatican II as a "danger" for the cohesion of the Protestant tradition, while confirming the exceptional theological and cultural shift operated by the council vis-à-vis the landscape of modern Christianity:

> The logic of the Second Vatican Council's overall position is to exert a kind of cognitive pressure on what I have just called "Reformation Protestants" to become more Catholic. To the degree that they become aware of the new possibilities introduced by the Council they are likely to think of themselves as Catholic exiles who now should be welcomed back into the Catholic communion, not despite but because of their Reformation heritage.[25]

An evolution can be seen also in the reactions of the Orthodox observers. At the beginning of the council in 1963, the Orthodox theologian (and member of the faculty of the St. Sergius Theological Orthodox Institute in Paris) Olivier Clément saw in Vatican II not more than mere "benevolence," and affirmed that there was no "truth" coming from the Catholic Church toward the Orthodox Church.[26] But later Clément's assessment adjusted in favor of a more positive view of the change happening at the council, especially concerning liturgy and ecclesiology.[27] The Greek Orthodox theologian Nikos Nissiotis (1925–86) saw the expression of an "ecclesial paternalism" at work at Vatican II, which acted as if the Catholic Church possessed every solution to the problems of human relations.[28] Nissiotis saw only some marginal differences between Vatican II and the traditional teaching of Catholicism on Scripture and tradition, the ecclesiology of the papacy, and the weak role of pneumatology. But, in the end, Nissiotis also appreciated Vatican II as a huge step forward in ecumenical relations and regretted the fact that Vatican II was overly cautious about the future of ecumenism. After Vatican II—Nissiotis said—it was time for a "pan-Christian" council of the Churches.

The ecumenical "observers" grasped with particular acumen the issue of change in the Catholic Church, the contribution of Vatican II to the rejuvenated life of the postconciliar Church, and the council as a watershed for Catholic theology. By examining the point of view of ecumenical observers, we see continuity between their perception of the theology of Vatican II and their predicament with the council's impact on the future of Catholicism: the observers took for granted the fact that change was happening in the Church after Vatican II. In some cases the observers were concerned about the impact on their own Churches, but none of them questioned the genuine power of change coming from within Vatican II and the reorientation of its theology around the sources of Scripture, tradition, and history. In the eyes of ecumenical observers, Vatican II changed the religious landscape of Christianity in a profound way: "Prior to the Council, the problems of Roman Catholicism were 'their' problems; now they are our problems. And, conversely, many of our problems have become theirs."[29]

CONCILIUM, COMMUNIO, AND POST–VATICAN II THEOLOGY

The ecumenical take on Vatican II—that is, the viewpoint of the ecumenical observers—represented the attitude of one side of the theological spectrum of Catholic theology that accepted Vatican II and helped shape its final documents. This view can be called an "incipial" theological interpretation of Vatican II (from the Latin *incipit*, "to begin"): a way to see Vatican II as an incipial moment, the beginning of a broad range of changes in the theology of the Catholic Church on the basis of the new orientation given by Vatican II to the relationship between theology and Scripture, tradition, and history.

The split between two tendencies within Catholic theology after Vatican II originated around this fault line. Both part and offspring of the best Catholic theological traditions of the twentieth century that had survived the antimodernistic purge under Pius X (*Pascendi Dominici Gregis*, 1907) and the doctrinal policy of Pius XII (*Humani generis*, 1950), the two schools gave life to the two most important theological journals founded after Vatican II: *Concilium* and *Communio*.

Concilium, the "International Journal for Theology" (published in English, Spanish, German, Portuguese, and Italian) was founded in 1964 by a group of theologians belonging to the conciliar majority, and including such names as Marie-Dominique Chenu, Yves Congar, Hans Küng, Karl Rahner, Edward Schillebeeckx, Joseph Ratzinger, and Henri de Lubac. The first issue of *Concilium* was published in January 1965. In the general introduction to the first issue (meaningfully devoted to the topic of dogma), Rahner and Schillebeeckx outlined the need for a new theological journal on the basis of the birth of a new theology that would surpass "the old manuals" and would be based on Scripture and the history of salvation:

50

"A new theology is taking shape....It is difficult to sketch even in outline the distinguishing marks of this new theology. Quite clearly, however, it is deliberately based on Scripture and the history of salvation....It seeks, on the basis of our contemporary situation, a better understanding of the Word of God for man and the world of our time." Rahner and Schillebeeckx went on to say that they did not seek for *Concilium*—marked by a clear intercultural, ecumenical, and critical approach—an exclusive interpretation of the theological legacy of Vatican II. They did, however, see the future of theology as a continuation of the work done by Vatican II, in an ecumenical direction and in other ways: "[T]he choice of this title means that the review will take cognizance of what the Church's pastoral authority, which was so remarkably expressed at Vatican II, has laid down as guidance for the faithful. Hence, in a special way, the review aims to continue the work of Vatican II."[30]

The differences *within* conciliar theology about the issue of change in theology—changes made by the council or to be made afterward—emerged soon after the years 1968 to 1970, with Paul VI's encyclical *Humanae vitae* on contraception, Hans Küng's book *The Church*,[31] and the Dutch Catechism.[32] These differences led to the creation of a second theological journal between 1969 and 1972, *Communio*, considered the theological rival of the journal *Concilium*.[33] Among the founders of *Communio* were theologians such as Hans Urs von Balthasar, Henri de Lubac, and Joseph Ratzinger, some of whom had previously been part of the board of *Concilium*. As Richard Gaillardetz put it: "These theologians shared a concern that the council's commitment to ecclesial renewal through a 'return to the sources' had been eclipsed by the postconciliar stress on aggiornamento and the reform of external structures."[34]

From a theological point of view, the founders of *Communio* were neo-Augustinians, convinced that *Concilium*'s emphasis on dialogue underplayed the revelation received by Christians in Christ. *Communio*'s emphasis on the biblical-theological concept of communion was portrayed by von Balthasar in the opening essay of the new journal as, in fact, antithetical to the idea of dialogue and communion advocated by "liberal" theologians:

> Strictly speaking, in the post-biblical era there are only two alternatives. One is Christian communion in the real principle of the divine Logos, who as conclusion and culmination of the Old Testament promise, has been bestowed on us in Jesus Christ, as grace yet in genuine humanity, making full communion possible. The other is evolutionary communism, which, spurred on by the passion of the forward-looking Old Testament hope, strives towards perfect community as the complete achievement of self-realization by the world-idea and humanity. It is clear that only in the first alternative is communion a really existent prior principle. In the second, communism remains, despite all striving towards it, merely ideal, and the means of forcibly compelling its achievement do not correspond to the basic spontaneity of "positive humanism."[35]

The theological fault lines between *Concilium* and *Communio* proved to have a long-lasting impact on post–Vatican II Catholic theology. The division of the conciliar majority into two separate groups and journals was the revealing moment of much tension already brewing during the council, though behind the curtains. The divisive issue was *Communio*'s idea of Vatican II as validating *ressourcement* as a method for further work in theology versus *Concilium*'s idea of Vatican II as the *incipit* of a *reformatio*, a more comprehensive updating of the

Catholic Church in its theology and structures.[36] These two interpretations of Vatican II also touched the political theology of Catholicism, and differed significantly in their evaluation of the theological consequences of the new ecclesiology for the social role of the Church in the Third World and the implementation of the new language of Catholic theology in non-Western Catholicism.

LIBERATION THEOLOGY AND FEMINIST THEOLOGY

The issue of change in Catholic theology at Vatican II and beyond Vatican II particularly affected the theological and sociopolitical standing of the Catholic Church in Latin America. Latin American Catholics taking part in Vatican II expressed the need for a theology that was socially more aware and politically more responsible on the basis of an ecclesiology of the "people of God" and of a biblical theology rooted in the idea of the history of salvation. The Latin American bishops, for example, voiced at Vatican II the connection between the "signs of the times" in the political and social situation of their Churches and the theology of the council. In March 1964, Brazil experienced a military coup d'état, but in the 1960s and 1970s, the entire Latin American subcontinent saw a series of military dictatorships, which invoked the threat of communism in the Cold War, and they sought the support of the Catholic Church in the fight.

In this political and social plight, the reception of Vatican II by Latin American Catholics was intertwined with the changing role of Catholicism in the continent. Vatican II had revealed the face of a more global Church, which, at the same time, was more engaged in the situation of the present times, that is, "the joys and the hopes, the griefs and the anxieties of the men of this age, especially those who are poor or in any way afflicted" (*Gaudium et spes* 1). The second assembly of the Latin American Episcopate in Medellín (1968) made clear the need for a coordinated and thoughtful implementation of Vatican II.[37] The period of 1968 to 1975 marked the age of the formulation of "liberation theology."

Between the beginning of the post–Vatican II period and the 1980s, Latin American theologians argued that Vatican II was the first part of a bridge formed by the council, Paul VI's encyclical *Populorum progressio* (1967), and the assembly of Medellín (1968). Thus, Latin American Catholic theology received Vatican II as the beginning of a new Catholic theology for the Church in Latin America:

> The Latin American Church, like the base-level ecclesial communities, the theologians of liberation, and Medellín, has made its own the insight of John XXIII vis-à-vis the Church of the poor, and it has tried to interpret the great themes of the Council in light of this insight. The statements made at Medellín and the program it laid out are inexplicable without reference to the Council in light of this insight.[38]

The 1968 assembly of Medellín was a unique experience in the global reception of Vatican II and the largest effort of a continental Church for a creative reception of the council. The criteria of this reception was a "faithful" reception of Vatican II together with a "creative" reception (initiating with the reality of the Latin American people as a sign of the times for the interpretation of the council); the final result was, as some of the most prominent Latin American theologians have acknowledged, a selective reception of the council, with an emphasis on ecclesiology, liturgy, and ecumenism, and with a marginal role for biblical theology.[39]

The third assembly of the Latin American bishops in Puebla (1979) reaffirmed Medellín's theological interpretation of Vatican II. The incipital interpretation of Vatican II as the beginning of a new theological assessment of the "signs of the times" was evident in the major works of the two "theologians of liberation"—the Spanish-born Jon Sobrino (1938–) and the Brazilian Leonardo Boff (1938–). Sobrino stated, as a point of departure for his theology of liberation, the ecclesiology of Vatican II: "The Church is the *people* of God. Any distinction between hierarchy and faithful is secondary."[40] Sobrino affirmed that this conception of the Church as a persecuted community, "partisan" for the poor, was consistent with the ecclesiology of Vatican II: "This Christian definition of 'persecution of the Church' will seem novel only to those who have failed to grasp what is new in the ecclesiology of Vatican II."[41]

The need for an ecclesiological implementation of Vatican II was evident also in the work of Leonardo Boff, who stressed the transitional character of Vatican II:

> Vatican Council II sought to strike a compromise between the two great ecclesiological currents of *communio* and *sacra potestas*, without, however, altering the outlines of the prevailing concept of ministry....Today we are confronted with practices which, while not *contra ordinem*, are indeed *praeter ordinem*. History has shown us that practices prevailing on the margins of the community order often finish by dynamizing that order, and conferring on it a new ecclesial expression that is later officially assimilated.[42]

Liberation theology originated from a particular historical and cultural setting, and it has remained not only in the
memory but also in the praxis of Latin American post–Vatican
II Catholicism, notwithstanding the official condemnations
from Rome starting in the mid-1980s. The legacy of liberation
theology is still working, and its impact has crossed geographical and methodological borders, embodying the most relevant
political-theological interpretation of Vatican II that had
already started during the council. At the end of the first age of
liberation theology (1968–75), Latin American theologians had
built a bridge toward other forms of liberation theology, such
as "black theology" and "feminist theology,"[43] so that by the
conference "Theology in the Americas" (Detroit, 1975), liberation theology had become a "plural"—liberation *theologies*.[44]

What indeed constituted a real step beyond the "letter" of
Vatican II was the development of a feminist theology on the
basis of the hermeneutical shift operated by the council. The
council fathers did not express interest in a gender-neutral theological language, and Vatican II as an event had as its main characters only male members of the clergy.[45] In 1965, a group of
women, led by Gertrud Heinzelmann, appealed to the council
fathers with the pamphlet *We Won't Keep Silence Any Longer:
Women Speak Out to Vatican Council II.*[46] In the wake of the Latin
American theology of liberation, feminist theology was born
(1971–72), and a comparable liberationist approach to Vatican II
emerged with the new wave of feminist theology, especially in
the United States, where the leading feminist theologians have
been Roman Catholics. The birth of Catholic feminist theology
was connected with the early years of the journal *Concilium* that
explored the theme of "women in the Church" in a special issue
in 1975, edited by the Catholic ecumenist Gregory Baum.[47] Ten
years later *Concilium* created a special section for feminist theology. Feminist theology interpreted the theology of Vatican II as

a far point of departure not only with respect to the issue of women in the Church, but also through a thoroughly ecumenical, interreligious, multicultural, and socio-political approach to the issue of the Church:

> In the past thirty years they [theological renewal movements] have attempted to turn the monarchic, exclusivist, and fundamentalist pre–Vatican II church into a church that would respect religious liberty, privilege the "option for the poor," and strive to reform Catholicism in light of the radical democratic vision of the people of G*d [*sic*]. Although the Second Vatican Council did not specifically wrestle with the problem of women, the ekklesial [*sic*] status of women is the linchpin for any such social and ekklesial [*sic*] reform program.[48]

A critical feminist theology of liberation did not challenge the authority of Vatican II, nor did it question its final documents, but it embodied a significant approach to the council in Catholic theology, especially in United States Catholicism. Within the stream of liberal feminism, two theologians stood out, Anne E. Carr (1934–2008) and Elizabeth A. Johnson (1941–), who in the 1970s participated in a "burgeoning feminist movement" and wrote "landmark works of Catholic feminist theology."[49] The works of Carr and Johnson rarely addressed Vatican II per se, but they clearly understood Vatican II as a provisional change—a much-to-be-augmented shift in Catholic theology. In Elizabeth Johnson's argument on the need to deconstruct the sexist reading of the Bible and the sexist language of theology, Vatican II clearly played the role of the beginning of a new theological framework for Catholic theology. In her ground-breaking book titled *She Who Is*,

Johnson connected the new hermeneutical framework for the study of the Bible given by *Dei Verbum* and *Gaudium et spes* in chapter 29 on the role of women in society:

> *Nostrae salutis causa*, "for the sake of our salvation." After much anguish and debate in the nineteenth century, and with implicit understanding, the slavery texts of the Bible were laid aside and no longer guide Christian discourse and behavior....The same dynamic now directs the interpretation of sexist biblical texts that in an analogous way can be judged according to the norm of whether they release salvation for the most abused women.[50]

The interpretation of the concept of tradition elaborated in *Dei Verbum* was crucial to the feminist reception of Vatican II: "This tradition which comes from the Apostles developed in the Church with the help of the Holy Spirit. For there is a growth in the understanding of the realities and the words which have been handed down" (*Dei Verbum* 8). This reading of *Dei Verbum* ("the growth in an understanding of the realities"), together with the ecclesiology of *Lumen Gentium* 12 ("the entire body of the faithful, anointed as they are by the Holy One"), expresses on one hand the plurality of the Church in terms of male and female, and on the other hand a changing understanding of the different components of the Church in terms of gender. This is the basis for the feminist's radical and creative interpretation of Vatican II.[51] Harriet Luckman, in the essay "Vatican II and the Role of Women," states: "The vision and accomplishments of Vatican II would have seemed outlandish and perhaps radical, if not also heretical, to Roman Catholics during the modernist crisis of the early 1900s. Perhaps an equally radical church will emerge from the post–Vatican II struggles of the twentieth and twenty-first century."[52] Symbol of one of the major rifts within Catholic post-conciliar theology, between an American gender-sensitive theological language on one side and the rest of Catholic theology on the other, feminist theology originated in the North American theological schools. In comparison to Latin American liberation theology and its dissemination in other areas of global Catholicism, feminist theology remained more confined to the North American area.

CATHOLIC THEOLOGY IN NEW PLACES: VATICAN II IN AFRICA, ASIA, AND AUSTRALASIA

Throughout its history, until the twentieth century, Christian theology had been mostly European theology with a North Atlantic extension. Vatican II gave theology new birthplaces: not only Latin America, but also Africa and Asia. Thanks to the theology of Vatican II on the local Church and on non-Christian religions, a theology of adaptation and inculturation took the place of the traditional theology of *salus animarum* (the "salvation of the souls") and the purely missionary theology of *plantatio ecclesiae* (the "expansion of the Church" and its structures).

A key passage in the history of the reception of Vatican II is the translation of a Catholic theology marked by its Greek, European, and Western cultural roots into a global culture. For Vatican II to be perceived as "the beginning" of a new era for Catholic theology, a crucial area of the reception of Vatican II was the non-European and non-Western experience of Vatican II in Africa, Asia, and Australasia:[53] Africa was the continent most marked by the history of the Christian missions and of the legacy of the cooperation between imperial colonialism and cultural colonialism; Asia, cradle of the great pre-Jewish and pre-Christian religions of India and China, posed a formidable theological challenge to Christian theology; Australia has a theological tradition that had developed little specifically by and for Australians, but its history with British colonization, its indigenous heritage, and its flow of immigrant populations made it one of the outposts of the globalized religious landscape. These three different continents acquired from Vatican II a clear right to develop an inculturated theology. For the history of Catholicism, the post–Vatican II period marks the beginning of these regional or continental theological traditions.

The history of the post–Vatican II Catholic Church and of the reception of Vatican II in Africa and Asia remains largely unwritten, or is confined to the perception of non-Western Catholicism as part of the global south of third-millennium Christianity.[54] But it is indisputable that Vatican II, the first truly global council, marked the beginning of a "World Church," and also with respect to the theological languages of the reception in a world shifting from a colonial to a postcolonial world order. After the significant contribution of the African bishops at Vatican II,[55] a series of theological conferences that took place in the mid-1970s in France highlighted the *déplacements*: the "displacement" of the centers for the elaboration of postconciliar theology from the Atlantic hemisphere to the southern and eastern parts of the world. The displacements concerned a new understanding of the sixteenth-century *loci theologici*, "places" or sources from which proofs are deduced in carrying out theology.[56] This diversification of the cultural and theological centers of global Catholicism became possible thanks to Vatican II, which the non-European Churches perceived as the beginning of a de-Europeanization of Catholic theology in a post-European and postcolonial world. At the same time, however, it is undeniable that some major contributions to Vatican II came from a firmly Western theological tradition, which was trying to demystify folk Catholicism and remove some points of contact between "pagan" devotions and Christianity.

The case of Africa has been particularly interesting for the reception of the council and in particular for the liturgical reform and the new link between Bible and liturgy. In a continent where decolonization coincided with the creation of a local Catholic hierarchy and with Vatican II and its reception, the theological implementation of the council was centered on the inculturation of Catholic theology into African culture. As witnessed by the contents of John Paul II's exhortation *Ecclesia in Africa* (1995) after the "Special Assembly for Africa of the Synod of Bishops" held in 1994, the focus of the African reception of Vatican II was on evangelization, inculturation, interreligious dialogue, ecumenism, and the socio-political role of the Church in the continent.[57]

From a pastoral point of view, Vatican II meant a more significant role for the use of the Bible in African theology and a notable change in liturgical style: "The most important single effect in Africa in popular terms of the Council has been the change in singing, in hymns, in music, in the use of musical instruments. The pre-Conciliar African church set its heart on the possession of a harmonium. The post-Conciliar African Church glories in its use of drums."[58] On the other side, the insufficient implementation of the ecclesiology of the people of God and the emphasis on the person of the priest have been recently identified, along with the lack of training in the reading of the Bible, as the major weaknesses of the reception of the council in Africa.[59] But the fundamental shift made possible by Vatican II was the birth of a truly African Christian discourse freed from the "circumcision" of the European Church, much as the Council of Jerusalem freed the Gentiles from the Mosaic Law (Acts 15).[60]

The African scenario was important thanks to the synchronized periodization between the celebration of Vatican II and the end of colonization. But even though the Asian religious landscape was much less touched by colonialism than the African one, the post–Vatican II period also meant for Asian Catholicism emancipation from missionary theology and the assumption of a new theological self-determination. The growth in the self-awareness of Asian Catholic theology was indeed impressive, the episcopate of which, during Vatican II, had been not as influential as the African episcopate (except for the Indian bishops).[61] Nevertheless, the issues had much in common with the post–Vatican II theology in Africa, in the interpretation of the future of the Asian Churches "with and beyond Vatican II."[62] According to Peter Phan, the reception of Vatican II in Asia began with the liturgical reform accompanied by an explicit effort of liturgical inculturation:

> Whereas the Catholic Church in Latin America has been more concerned with the socio-economic oppression of the poor and marginalized, and hence was more focused on *liberation*, Asian Christians, while also concerned with the issues of justice, have been more engaged in the *inculturation* of the Christian faith.[63]

The crucial role of *Gaudium et spes* in the debate on the hermeneutics of the council originated (although not exclusively) from the role played by the pastoral constitution in the theological discourse about liberation and inculturation that shaped the early post-Vatican II theology of the Catholic "global south." To make an interesting comparison, while the Latin American reception of *Gaudium et spes* centered on the Church in social and political life (paragraphs 63 to 76), the Asian reception focused on the development of culture in the world of today (paragraphs 54 to 62).

The growth of an Asian theology was accompanied by the creation of the Federation of Asian Bishops' Conferences between 1970 and 1972, considered "a landmark in the history of Christianity in Asia."[64] The Asian post–Vatican II theology had as constitutive dimensions the dialogue with other religions in the first place, and ecumenical dialogue in the second place. Moreover, the newly discovered awareness of the original and not derived character of Asian Christianity (in the Middle East, in India, and in China alike) entailed huge theological challenges for Catholic theology. In terms of ecclesiology, this new awareness demanded a more decentralized ecclesiology, less dependent on the medieval and Tridentine forms of Church governance. From the point of view of the whole theological balance, the religious landscape of Asia, in which Christianity is a minority against the background of religious traditions that precede the Judeo-Christian tradition, required a shift from an ecclesio-centric mission to a missionary Church whose goal was the kingdom.[65] This was accompanied by theological research for a new Christology and a new understanding of the relationship between Christ and the pre-Christian religions, which created tensions between some major Asian theologians and the Vatican, starting in the 1990s.[66] But, more generally, at the center of the Asian reception of Vatican II was the issue of the "Asianness" of the Church—not a Church *in* Asia, but a Church *of* Asia. As stated at the Asian Bishops' Conferences in 1977, Vatican II in Asia meant the development of "genuine Christian communities in Asia—Asian in their way of thinking, praying, living, communicating their own Christ-experience to others."[67]

Geographically close to the Asian world, but culturally much less willing to renounce the Western heritage of Catholic theology, the specifically Australian contribution to the debate about Vatican II is more difficult to identify. The Australian bishops were active at Vatican II, but more as active recipients of the message of the council than makers of what was occurring.[68] Nevertheless, they were one of the first English-speaking bishops' conferences to accept during the council the vernacular breviary and to introduce guidelines for liturgy in both English and Latin. Similar to the occurrences in the rest of world Catholicism, for the Church in Australia, the post–Vatican II period meant a new engagement with social justice and human rights research, advocacy, education, the plight of refugees, asylum seekers, and indigenous reconciliation. Nevertheless, it is worth noting that some authors have identified in Australia in the 1980s the beginning of a division between Catholics: those with a sense of "Catholic nostalgia," and those convinced that reform and renewal had not gone far enough, especially in terms of the impact of feminism and the growth of democratic and collegial decision making. Thus, the Australian case became similar to the polarization of American and European Catholicism between a "liberal" majority (those who saw Vatican II as the beginning of a new flourishing) and a "conservative" minority (those who saw Vatican II as the beginning of the decline of Catholicism and of its absorption into secular culture).[69]

The Australian case—far beyond the historical boundaries of an ancien régime, European, missionary Catholicism—represents a telling epilogue of the first period of the global reception of Vatican II, together with the liberationist and feminist receptions of Vatican II. The debate within the Australian Church around Vatican II was similar to what happened in other Churches, but it also embodied a kind of rebound effect after the first period of the implementation. In other areas this rebound effect constituted the early end of the attempts of non-Western and more creative and radical Catholic theologies to "own Vatican II," spelled out by their decision to follow a different path: not anticonciliar, but less directly engaged with the issue of the interpretation of Vatican II.

This result came as a consequence of the very narrow limits set by post–Vatican II doctrinal policy in terms of creativity and of the protagonism of local Churches, non-Western Churches, and women's theology. At the 1985 Synod of Bishops on the reception of Vatican II, it had become clear that the debate about the significance of the council was a hermeneutically divisive issue for the Catholic Churches of the Western world; in contrast, Catholic Churches from Africa, Asia, and Latin America and feminist theology had taken a different path, which was neglected and soon forgotten by the center of world Catholicism.

4

THE CHURCH AND THE WORLD: AUGUSTINIANS AND THOMISTS

FROM VATICAN II TO POST–VATICAN II: THE NEW "TWO TENDENCIES"

As we move closer to the theological receptions of Vatican II during John Paul II's pontificate, we approach a twofold debate on a core issue of the council: the relationship between the Church and the world. It is not an overstatement to affirm that this issue was the origin of a major rift in the interpretations of the council, a rift much more visible after the council than during the council.

For too much time, the debate between different interpretations of Vatican II has been framed—especially in the media—as a clash between liberal or progressive Catholics on one side and conservative Catholics on the other. Far from denying the existence of different ideological orientations in contemporary Catholicism, a sound assessment of theology since Vatican II should note that the roots of different kinds of reception are to be found primarily not in political or ideological affiliations, nor in the existence of a "theological theology" opposed to a Roman Curia "doctrinal policy," but in theolog-

66

ical views about Christology and ecclesiology and, more profoundly, in a theological (and philosophical) divide between neo-Augustinians (philosophically close to Platonism) and neo-Thomists (philosophically close to Aristotelians).[1]

The gap between two streams of interpretation of the major theological issues of Vatican II is far from an invention of post–Vatican II historians. From the very beginning of Vatican II, the council was aware of the development of two main tendencies. During the council, Gérard Philips, Belgian theologian and joint secretary to the Doctrinal Commission of Vatican II, effectively described in an early essay the split between the majority and the minority:

> The presence of two tendencies in the doctrinal life of the Church, the first eager to remain faithful to a more traditional message, the second more worried about the spread of the message to contemporary man, is a permanent and normal phenomenon. But at certain moments in the history of theological thought the confrontation between them can provoke much more vibrant discussions and turn out to be a conflict.[2]

Philips advocated the necessity of returning to the sources of the Church fathers, theological *ressourcement*, without overlooking the contribution of Scholastic theology, Thomas Aquinas, and Aristotelian philosophy. According to Philips, avoiding this theological-cultural evolution would be dangerous and especially unrealistic; theological *ressourcement* was an urgent yet challenging task: as he stated, "Transformation, it is true, does not come without pain."[3]

Philips wrote this famous article in early 1963, and his interpretation of the positioning of theological schools at Vatican II has been insightful and long-lasting. After Philips' article, from the first intersession of spring–summer 1963 to December 1965, the council unfolded and modified its internal dynamics, especially between the *aula* of St. Peter and the new pope, Paul VI (elected June 21, 1963). It is therefore necessary to look beyond the early interpretation of the "two tendencies" to the new face of this rift, which we could now call the neo-Augustinians/neo-Thomists "fault line," following the interpretation given by Joseph Komonchak.[4]

It is far from a bold assessment to say that there are again two new tendencies in Catholic theology about Vatican II: the major rift in the interpretations of Vatican II constitutes the separation around the issue of the role of a "patristic-monastic and Augustinian theology" versus a "neo-Thomistic theology." The different conceptions of the pivotal role of the former or the latter cast a light on the broader issue of the relationship between the Church and the world in the debate about Vatican II. This feature of the debate became more visible and received important theological assessments both during and after the 1985 Extraordinary Synod of Bishops concerning the reception of the council.

NEO-AUGUSTINIAN RECEPTIONS OF VATICAN II

The interpretation of the relationship between modern culture and Christian anthropology is at the center of the divide between the two tendencies. The neo-Augustinian tendency on one side, and the communitarian or neo-Thomist school on the other, have been described recently in relation to the different anthropologies necessary for a correct "hermeneutics of the authors" of Vatican II. In the words of Ormond Rush: "The Augustinian school is wanting to set church and world in a situation of rivals; it sees the world in a negative light; evil and sin so abound in the world that the church should be always suspicious and distrustful of it. Any openness to the world would be 'naive optimism.'"[5] In Avery Dulles's description, the neo-Augustinian tendency views the Church as far removed from a sinful world, with "the Church as an island of grace in a world given over to sin."[6]

This tendency attracted many theologians, and not only those members of the purely conservative party within twentieth-century Catholicism; some theologians already have been mentioned, as eminent representatives of the *nouvelle théologie* or of the *ressourcement* of twentieth-century Catholic theology. Joseph Ratzinger, Henri de Lubac, Jean Daniélou, Hans Urs von Balthasar, and Louis Bouyer shared a common affinity for a monastic, medieval, neo-Augustinian theology and kept a resolute distance from a neo-Thomistic interpretation of the *aggiornamento* of Vatican II.

The centrality of Augustine is quite visible in theologians whose stance toward Vatican II could be defined as skeptical if not critical. However, the intellectual biography of many neo-Augustinian critics of Vatican II has been far more complex than the advocacy of a merely conservative agenda. For example, the Augustinianism of Hans Urs von Balthasar (1905–88) is visible in his analysis of post–Vatican II Catholicism. Nevertheless, in his book *Razing the Bastions*, published some ten years before the council, von Balthasar expressed the need for the Church to no longer be "barricaded" against the world.[7] After the council, the same von Balthasar saw only the first half of this openness to the world, the conciliar *aggiornamento*. The second half was still to be accomplished. "The other half is a reflection on the specifically Christian element itself, a purification, a deepening, a centering of its idea, which alone renders us capable of representing it, radiating it, translating it believably in the world."[8]

In the final analysis, von Balthasar, reflecting on *Razing the Bastions* concerning the relationship between the Church and the modern world, wrote: "That impatient blast of the trumpet calling for a Church no longer barricaded against the world...did not die away unheard, but now it forced the trumpeter himself to reflect more deeply."[9] Nevertheless, Vatican II left a mark on von Balthasar's wish for a more open Church. In his judgment, the period between 1965 and 1975 saw a radical shift in the relationship between theology and culture. He saw in some aspects of post–Vatican II theology the result of a marriage between English deism (Herbert of Cherbury) and German historicism and idealism (Hegel) at the expense of Thomas Aquinas: "This [postconciliar period] is the christening of the Enlightenment and of liberal theology from Herbert of Cherbury down to the present day....This is the christening of German Idealism, into whose transcendental key even the metaphysical thinking of St. Thomas can be transposed."[10]

In the mid-1970s, von Balthasar's defense of the papacy against what he called a "disturbing" phenomenon of anti-Roman sentiment developing after Vatican II was centered on Augustine's ecclesiology. Seeing in the contemporary anti-Roman attitude a modern version of such early heresies as Donatism and Montanism, von Balthasar stressed the importance of Augustine's ecclesiology: "Augustine's concept of the Church is sufficiently flexible (without falling apart) to see the innermost essence of the Church in the pure community of love."[11]

Von Balthasar was the most conspicuous example of Catholic theologians who were not present at the debates of Vatican II and who kept some distance from the fierce discussion raging in post–Vatican II Catholicism. But the analysis of the neo-Augustinian tendency helps in interpreting the role of de Lubac and, in particular, Ratzinger, whose position had a profound impact on the history of theology after the council.

The skepticism of Henri de Lubac (1896–1991) toward the anthropology of Vatican II, and of *Gaudium et spes* especially, was already evident during the council. We see this as we browse through the pages of his "conciliar journal" between 1964 and 1965 and in the debate about the final drafts of the pastoral constitution, in which de Lubac expressed harsh judgments about the fundamental orientations, if not the very basic theological knowledge, of some prominent leaders of the conciliar majority.[12] De Lubac's perception of Vatican II shared nothing with the Lefebvrian rejection of the council, as de Lubac remained always loyal to Vatican II as a legitimate council of the Catholic Church; but his perception of Vatican II as a "surrender" to an excessive optimism about the modern world would only grow in the years to come. In the "Introduction" to *Augustinisme et théologie moderne* (1971), de Lubac wrote: "Today we are witnesses of an endeavour that wants to dissolve the Church into the world....The tide of immanentism is growing irresistibly."[13] De Lubac developed an analysis of the post–Vatican II period as a time in which the theological balance between nature and grace had been disrupted in favor of a naive confidence in nature and the world against the need of grace and faith, and against the idea of transcendence. But de Lubac also saw a dissonance between the "council" on one side and the "para-council" on the other—a distinction that many others adopted after him:

> Just as the Second Vatican Council received from a number of theologians instructions about various points of the task it should assume, under pain of "disappointing the world," so too the "post-conciliar" Church was immediately and from all sides assailed with summons to get in step, not with what the

Council had actually said, but with what it should have said.[14]

Immediately before the 1985 synod, Henri de Lubac repeated his view of the post–Vatican II situation as an unprecedented crisis in the history of Catholic theology and stressed the need to avoid in the interpretation of Vatican II the "analogical interpretation" of the documents of the council. De Lubac described the relationship between Vatican I and Vatican II in unequivocal terms: "Vatican II completed the work initiated by Vatican I…through a solemn teaching that confirms the teaching of the whole Catholic Tradition."[15] For that matter, de Lubac's positive judgment of Karol Wojtyla's interventions in the subcommittee about atheism during the drafting of *Gaudium et spes* only foreshadowed the influence of de Lubac's views on the future John Paul II.[16]

But Joseph Ratzinger's appreciation of Wojtyla's anthropology was even more important than de Lubac's influence on John Paul II's pontificate and on the history of the debate about Vatican II. Ratzinger agreed with much of de Lubac's views about the postconciliar situation, but as a cardinal prefect of the Congregation for the Doctrine of the Faith from 1981 to 2005—and as pope after his election in April 2005—Ratzinger had many more opportunities to enforce his judgment. As a matter of fact, Ratzinger's Augustinianism dates back to his years in high school, in Nazi-ruled Germany, when the idea of a "City of God" worked as an antidote to the political and ethical totalitarianism that was ruling Germany, including Catholic Bavaria.[17] But it is his postdoctoral work on Bonaventure that helps in understanding Ratzinger's future overall assessment of the anthropology and ecclesiology of Vatican II and his evolution from young theologian pushing for renewal—as *peritus* of Cardinal Frings of Cologne during

Vatican II—to the pointed reviewer of Vatican II from the early 1970s.[18] From the very beginning of the post–Vatican II period, Ratzinger stressed the importance of a correct interpretation of the new openness to other Christians and to the problems of humankind. The council was not a cheap adaptation to a world mentality, but rather a profound retrieval of the very source of theology—that is, the missionary duty toward the world.[19] Ratzinger's judgment of Vatican II focused on the role of *Gaudium et spes*;[20] in particular, it mirrored his proximity to Augustine's pessimism about human freedom and, in general, the rejection of a Thomist epistemology in favor of a more kerygmatic vision of Christian faith.[21]

Quite significantly, Ratzinger structured the epilogue of his *Principles of Catholic Theology* in two chapters: "Review of the Postconciliar Era—Failures, Tasks, Hopes," and "Church and World." In this last chapter, Ratzinger reaffirmed the need to demythologize the 1960s and to limit the myth that the council was just about discerning the "signs of the times," a view he had first expressed in the mid-1970s:

> Something of the Kennedy era pervaded the Council, something of the naïve optimism of the concept of the great society. It was precisely the break in historical consciousness, the self-tormenting rejection of the past, that produced the concept of a zero hour in which everything would begin again and all those things that had formerly been done badly would now be done well.[22]

Given this view, it is clear why the pastoral constitution *Gaudium et spes*, concerning the Church and the modern world, is at the center of Ratzinger's critique: as he states, "The lack of clarity that persists even today about the real meaning of Vatican II is closely associated with such diagnosis and, consequently, with this document."[23] He followed this by saying that the affirmations in *Gaudium et spes* "breathe an astonishing optimism," resulting in nothing more than "a revision of the *Syllabus* of Pius IX, a kind of counter-syllabus," which was intended to reverse the negative stance adopted by Pius IX against the political and doctrinal "errors" of modernity listed in the *Syllabus* of 1864.[24]

Ratzinger's Augustinianism is at the basis not only of his judgment of *Gaudium et spes* (a judgment he shared, in 1965, with other German theologians at Vatican II, such as Karl Rahner), but also his views about the theology of liberation and the political theology of Jürgen Moltmann and Johann Baptist Metz. Ratzinger's assumption that the dualism between the "kingdom of God" and the "order of history" is essential to the core of Christian faith comes from his post-doctoral work on Bonaventure and shapes much of his overall assessment of Vatican II. Nevertheless, his view of the theological roots of Vatican II puts him at odds with a widespread perception of the "modernity" of the council. Ratzinger fought the assumption of "liberal" theologians about the reconciliation between Catholic theology and modernity by reminding them of the "roots" of the theological reorientation of Vatican II, that is, the fathers of the Church:

> Today it is being said with increasing frequency that the Council thereby placed itself under the aegis of the European Enlightenment. But the Council Fathers had a different motive for their orientation; they derived it from the theology of the Fathers of the Church, where St. Augustine, for example, strongly emphasized the difference between Christian simplicity and the empty pomp of pagan liturgies.[25]

74

The Church and the World: Augustinians and Thomists

Ratzinger's defense of Augustinianism was matched, during the years in which he formed a harsh opinion of Vatican II, by the impression that the defenders of Scholastic theology at the council had soon surrendered to a kind of new modernism. Ratzinger saw this new modernism in the adoption of a "utopian interpretation" of Vatican II, tied ultimately to a "theology of the world."[26]

"PROGRESSIVE" NEO-THOMISTS

A second fundamental tendency in the interpretation of Vatican II can be called post–Vatican II Thomism. The specification "post–Vatican II" is necessary given the complicated history of the relations among Thomist theologians at Vatican II. As Rush explains:

> The formerly united progressive group of post-Scholastic Thomists, having rejected the Thomism of neo-Scholasticism, have now divided, forming two groups in the aula: 1) a new "progressive" group wanting to retrieve a re-interpreted Thomism, and counseling openness to the world, and 2) a new "conservative" group wanting to retrieve the Augustinian vision, and counseling caution in the church's relationship to the world.[27]

While the second group had become much more Augustinian than Thomist, "reinterpreted Thomism" represented the other side of the debate concerning the Church and the modern world. This group of "progressive Thomists" included Yves Congar, Marie-Dominique Chenu, and Edward Schillebeeckx— Dominican theologians who had survived not only the pre–

Vatican II repression against the "new theology," but also the internal struggle concerning the approach to Thomism that had started in the 1940s: "The organized movement can be said to have reached its end by the time of the Second Vatican Council."[28] With these Dominicans, the Jesuits Karl Rahner and Bernard Lonergan shared a fundamentally Thomistic epistemology. The 1989 historical assessment made by Gerald McCool, the Fordham historian of Thomism, recognizes the contribution of a Thomism that defends the place of history and pluralism in theology: "During and after the Second Vatican Council, the 'new theologians' were counted among the leading theologians in the Church and their disciples became the leaders of the generation of theologians who succeeded them."[29]

A positive appreciation of history as a tool for theological work was at the center of the theology of the neo-Thomists. In his pre–Vatican II research, the French Dominican Marie-Dominique Chenu (1895–1990) proposed a fundamental historicization of the theology of Thomas Aquinas—that twentieth-century Catholic theology should do with modern philosophy and social sciences what Thomas had done with Aristotle in the thirteenth century, but now based on a new view of the relationship between faith and history, of the primacy of revelation in Scripture.[30] History and pluralism were at the center of Chenu's contribution to the debate at Vatican II, as is visible in his judgment of the preparatory schema on original sin (October 1962): "The schema, drafted by Fr. Trapé, is constructed exclusively within Latin theology and, in this frame, it also has a hyper-Augustinian tone."[31] Chenu's emphasis on the "signs of the times" in the interpretation of Vatican II and especially of *Gaudium et spes* was the consistent reading of the new facts in Vatican II Catholicism as theological sources, as "*loci theologici* in act": the missionary expansion, the pluralism of human civilizations, the ecumenical movement, and the apostolate of the laity.[32] Chenu's view of the "signs of the times" was consistent with an actualization of Thomas' theology:

> Given that the "sacred doctrine" does not present itself as a system of abstract principles whose application depends from a mental or moral casuistry, but, according to St. Thomas, as the Word of God developing itself within human intelligence in the act of faith, the "signs of the times" must enter, implicitly or explicitly, in the discernment of the impact of the Word in the historical community of the faithful.[33]

The distance between Chenu and the Augustinians is clear when we consider Chenu's assumption that the distinction between sin and grace "was inadequate on Thomist grounds because it neglected the created autonomy and intelligibility of the world of nature, man and history, and because it tended to compromise the methodological autonomy of the sciences that study it."[34] Therefore, understanding the *aggiornamento* of the Church that was achieved at Vatican II required understanding Christianity both in its dimension of "theology in act" and in its development that only with the help of the social sciences could theology perceive the "signs of the times." For Chenu, the interpretation of Vatican II was inextricable from the perception of "the end of the Constantine era," that is, the end of the strict accord between the Altar and the Throne, between the Church and the State: this phenomenon not only was a change in the historical and cultural situation of western Christianity, but it also required a change in the relationship between theology and history.[35]

77

Gaudium et spes had a similar importance in the interpretation of Vatican II according to the Dominican Dutch theologian Edward Schillebeeckx, whose inspiring principle was that Vatican II made possible the rediscovery of Christianity as an "event," thanks also to a new belief in man. As Schillebeeckx put it: "The renewed self-awareness of the church and the new, human and Christian appraisal of the world demand that the church redefine its position toward the secularized world. To this new appraisal Schema 13 [*Gaudium et spes*] must solemnly bear witness."[36] Schillebeeckx's "progressive" Thomism was visible in the positive appreciation of modern philosophy. In his commentary on the decree on training for the priesthood he wrote:

> The studies are to start off with a global initiation in salvation history, a kind of overall saving-historical picture of the redemptive mystery in which we are living. This is followed by philosophy, which must, in its contents at least, be synchronized with theology. Philosophy must be centered on man, his world and God.[37]

The French Dominican Yves Congar (1905–95), one of the most important, if not *the* most important theologian of the council, focused more on the relevance of history for theology.[38] His interpretation of the relationship between Thomism and modern theology started at the seminary of Le Saulchoir in Etiolles, near Paris, where he focused on historical theology, and which continued with the publication of his fundamental works in the pioneering years of ecumenism.[39]

Congar spent difficult years in the Dominican order because of the repression of the "new theology" and because of his being curtailed during Pius XII's pontificate.[40] Nevertheless, Congar's complicated relationship with the General Curia of the

Dominican order and with other Dominican theologians (like Michel Labourdette) did not distance him from Aquinas's theology. During the first session of Vatican II, Congar visited southern Italy, not far from Aquinas's birthplace, and entered in his journal: "What I see makes me understand why St. Thomas was so attentive to Arabs and gentiles. I imagine a St. Thomas very attentive, open and active towards the world he was facing."[41] One year later, Congar remembered the Dominican school of theology at Le Saulchoir as offering "a theology at the service of the Church for the needs of its time, according to St. Thomas's mission."[42] But Congar's neo-Thomism made him very critical of neo-Scholasticism. Toward the end of the Council, Congar criticized the extreme attempt by the Roman Curia to reintroduce neo-Scholastic theology as the rule for Catholic schools and universities: "It would be just like using Thomas Aquinas against himself."[43]

Congar's neo-Thomism never blinded him to the historicity of Thomas's theology and the need to adopt Thomas's approach rather than his conclusions. Congar's appreciation of Vatican II ecclesiology could not escape the duty of finding the need for an implementation of Aquinas's ecclesiology, especially concerning the idea of the "Church as a communion" and the lack of a developed theology of episcopacy and episcopal collegiality.[44]

Through the battles that made Vatican II such an epochal event—on episcopal collegiality, ecumenism, ecclesiology, and divine revelation—and through the post–Vatican II era, Congar always remained in the arena fighting for a profound renewal of Catholic theology. At the beginning of John Paul II's pontificate, Congar expressed the conviction that Vatican II had been primarily an "event." Congar's reading of Vatican II firmly denied that the council was at the origin of the crisis of postconciliar Catholicism:

I do not believe that the present crisis is the fruit of Vatican II. On the one hand, much of the disturbing facts we see today were on their way already in the 1950s, sometimes already in the 1930s. Vatican II has been followed by a socio-cultural mutation whose amplitude, radicality, rapidity, and global character have no equivalent in any other period in history. The Council felt this mutation, but it did not know every aspect nor its violence.[45]

Congar believed that Vatican II had achieved something similar to what the Thomist revolution had achieved in the thirteenth century, but most of all he perceived the institutional revolution carried out by the council:

Thanks to *Gaudium et spes* and to the declaration on religious freedom [*Dignitatis humanae*], Vatican II, which quoted often St. Augustine, managed to free the Church from the "political Augustinianism." We know that "political Augustinianism" is a position that makes the validity of structures and temporal activities depend from their conformity to a supernatural justice presupposing faith and love. The Albertine-Thomist revolution had produced, in this system, a theologically decisive gap. In the same way, Vatican II offers an act of pastoral magisterium that engages the whole church.[46]

A similar neo-Thomist view of theology after Vatican II was shared by Karl Rahner (1904–84). Rahner's view of Vatican II as "the beginning of a beginning" of a new era—that is, of Catholicism as a "World Church"—was nevertheless faithful to the idea of the necessity of a philosophical backbone for contemporary theology. Before the end of Vatican II Rahner wrote:

> The turning from a cosmocentric objective philosophy of the Greeks to the anthropocentric transcendental philosophy of the moderns is perfectly Christian in principle and basically already begins with St. Thomas; [but] the ecclesiastical "philosophy of the schools" has still much to catch up on and to save with regard to what has been developed apart from it.[47]

Rahner did not see the necessity of a change in the relationship between theology and philosophy; rather, he saw the need for a change in the cultural identity of philosophy, and especially in the cultural self-understanding of the Church as a "World Church" (and not as a "Western Church" anymore):

> The West need not abandon its own synthesis of theology and philosophy in favour of an attempt to hand on the, as it were, naked message of Christianity without the so-called "overlay" of Western philosophy. This does not mean, however, that the Western world should be allowed to extend its traditional philosophy in a traditional way into a world-philosophy.[48]

More focused on Thomas's doctrine of grace and theory of knowledge was the Canadian Jesuit Bernard Lonergan (1904–84), who prepared Catholic theology for an encounter with modern science (in his book *Insight*) and with modern social sciences (in *Method in Theology*).[49] After his revolutionary reading of Thomas Aquinas, Lonergan saw in Vatican II a shift from a "classicist" culture to a world marked by "historical

consciousness." In 1968, while talking about the future of
Thomism, Lonergan affirmed:

> As in our day there is a demand for an *aggiornamento*
> of our thinking, so in his there was a demand for an
> *aggiornamento* of earlier medieval thought....A
> Thomism for tomorrow will involve first a shift
> from the emphases of classical Thomism and, sec-
> ondly, a revision of the results obtained by medieval
> theology.[50]

Lonergan was one of the most important examples of an evolution in Vatican II Thomism, that is, a neo-Thomist reading
of theology and culture in the Vatican II era:

> This development necessitates a complete restructur-
> ing of Catholic theology, for the deductivist approach
> of the past was possible only as long as accurate and
> detailed knowledge was lacking. While Scholastic cat-
> egories are being replaced by more relevant categories
> drawn from historicist, phenomenological, existential-
> ist, and personalist trends, there is occurring a shift, in
> Karl Rahner's terminology, from a cosmological to an
> anthropological viewpoint.[51]

Lonergan's contribution to the debates about Vatican II
was not comparable to Chenu's or Congar's. Nevertheless,
Lonergan was not any less aware of the necessity of the change
brought about by Vatican II:

> They are changes, not in God's self-disclosure or our
> faith, but in our culture. They are changes such as
> occurred when the first Christians moved from
> Palestine into the Roman Empire...when Scho-

lasticism yielded to Humanism, the Renaissance, the Reformation and the Counter-reformation. Ours is a new age, and enormous tasks lie ahead. But we shall be all the more likely to surmount them, if we take the trouble to understand what is going forward and why.[52]

THE DEBATE AT THE 1985 SYNOD

Between November 24 and December 8, 1985, 165 bishops representing the episcopal conferences (and in part appointed by John Paul II) discussed the role of Vatican II in the postconciliar Church, and developed some principles for the reception of the council. The 1985 Extraordinary Synod of Bishops is a significant landmark in the history of the debate about the council, despite the fact that, as one observer remarked, "from a procedural and structural viewpoint, the Extraordinary Synod of 1985 presents a good many anomalies."[53]

Pope John Paul II had announced the convening of this "extraordinary session" of the Synod of Bishops only ten months before—on January 25, 1985—exactly twenty-six years after John XXIII's announcement of Vatican II. The synod was called in order to celebrate the event of Vatican II and to evaluate the "application" of the council in the past twenty years. In preparation, the general secretariat of the synod sent the patriarchs and the presidents of the bishops' conferences a questionnaire; the responses were to be used for the preparation of the initial report. According to Alberto Melloni, the questions were in many ways suggestive of the intention of John Paul II: "Many of these particular questions contained the presupposition that the Synod would demonstrate the limits of the reception of Vatican II." Melloni goes on to say that in the short period of time given (six months), the general secretariat received back 95 replies out of a possible 136: "Nearly all the responses distanced themselves from the negative tone of part of the questionnaire of the secretary general and also from J. Ratzinger's hypotheses."[54]

In many ways the bishops' replies *before* the synod are its "most enduring fruit,"[55] because many notions developed by Vatican II were suppressed or silenced when the bishops convened. One such notion was the "people of God":

> Somewhere between the Council and the Synod, it came to be believed that to stress the mystery of the Church required one to underplay the Church as the People of God, to the point that some observers even speak of the Synod's having "entombed" the expression "People of God." Neither the pre-synodal responses nor the synodal interventions required this development.[56]

Nevertheless, for the history of the debate on Vatican II, the impact of the final report was much more long-lasting than the preparatory consultation of the bishops.

In its final report, the synod came up with six principles for sound interpretation of Vatican II, which Avery Dulles paraphrased as follows:

1. Each passage and document of the Council must be interpreted in the context of all the others, so that the integral meaning of the Council may be rightly grasped.

2. The four major constitutions of the Council are the hermeneutical key for the other decrees and declarations.

3. The pastoral import of the documents may not be separated from, or set in opposition to, their doctrinal content.

4. No opposition may be made between the spirit and the letter of Vatican II.

5. The Council must be interpreted in continuity with the great tradition of the Church, including earlier councils.

6. Vatican II must be accepted as illuminating the problems of our own day.[57]

The credit for the synod's final report, *relatio finalis*, was given to Cardinal Godfried Danneels (bishop of Malines-Brussels, Belgium) and to the German theologian and secretary of the synod, Walter Kasper (appointed cardinal in 2001). Kasper's ecclesiological interpretation of Vatican II was visible in the opening of the *relatio*, in which Vatican II was defined as a "grace of God and a gift of the Holy Spirit, from which have come forth many spiritual fruits *for the universal Church and the particular Churches*, as well as for the men of our time."[58] From a historical point of view, the reading of the reception of Vatican II was much closer to the "optimism" of the council itself than to the "skepticism" that many Catholic bishops and theologians later felt toward the council at the beginning of the twenty-first century, despite the visible "reversals" imposed by the 1985 Synod of Bishops on how Vatican II ecclesiology had already been received between 1965 and 1985.

The *relatio* of the synod addressed the interpretation of *Gaudium et spes* and emphasized the theory and practice of inculturation and the dialogue with non-Christian religions and nonbelievers. The *relatio* proposed a more visible role for the theology of the cross in preaching and in theology itself, thus expressing a less optimistic view of the relationship between the Church and the world. But it did not advocate an interpretation of the pastoral constitution that was detached from the "signs of the times." As the *relatio* states: "The signs of our time are in part different from the time of the council, with greater problems and anguish."[59]

The change in perspective about the Church and the world made the synod a turning point for the rise of the neo-Augustinian reception of Vatican II within the doctrinal orientation of the pontificate of John Paul II. It is correct to see in the role of the pastoral constitution *Gaudium et spes* and in its anthropology many of the roots of the disagreements in post–Vatican II Catholicism: the neo-Augustinian theologians played a major role in challenging a complaisant reading of Vatican II in its relationship with the modern world and "terrestrial realities," especially as they were addressed in *Gaudium et spes* 54–62.

The 1985 Extraordinary Synod of Bishops marked an important milestone because it represented the first major attempt of John Paul II's pontificate to steer the reception of Vatican II in a direction that he desired. As archbishop of Krakow, the pope himself had been a conciliar father and an active participant in the debates in St. Peter and in the conciliar commission for the drafting of *Gaudium et spes*. The synod reflected some features of his style, and the final results of the synod revealed the complexity of his interpretation of Vatican II: a clear development in the issues *ad extra* (social teaching, ecumenism, interreligious dialogue) and a more conservative approach to the issues *ad intra*. That complexity had become apparent already in the final steps of the 1983 Code of Canon Law, which assembled with a great deal of "ambiguity" two different elements, that is, the mainly Tridentine and juridical ecclesiology of *societas* and the more theological ecclesiology of *communio*.[60]

In the debates at the synod and in its final documents, it was clearly possible to see that some theological decisions made by Vatican II had been revised and reinterpreted by John Paul II. The notion of the Church as a "people of God" lost the momentum it had gained twenty years before at the council. The idea of a "universal catechism," set aside by the council, was revived, thanks to the suggestion coming from some episcopal conferences (including those of the United States, Korea, Senegal, and Burundi), and thus opened the way for the *Catechism of the Catholic Church* published by the Holy See in 1992. The *relatio* distinguished between episcopal collegiality and its "partial realizations," such as the Synod of Bishops, the episcopal conferences, the Roman Curia, the *ad limina* visits, and so on, attempting to limit the scope of collegiality to the relationship between the pope and the bishops. The role of episcopal conferences, while evidently reinforced by the process of the reception of Vatican II and by the very Rome-centered mechanics of the Synod of Bishops, was decisively reduced to a mere tool and deprived of real ecclesiological meaning. This "institutional reception" of Vatican II by the Roman Curia was embodied and led by the theological views that Cardinal Ratzinger had expressed in his 1985 best-seller, *The Ratzinger Report*, and later confirmed in the 1986 report of the International Theological Commission, which was chaired by him.[61]

The final report of the 1985 Extraordinary Synod of Bishops reflected some of the tensions that had emerged in the global reception of Vatican II after 1965, but also revealed and cemented the long-lasting effects of the diverging hermeneutical tendencies present in post–Vatican II Catholicism. The theologian Gilles Routhier of Université Laval in Quebec correctly saw a crucial moment in the synod, in that it was "the beginning of a process of gradual but sure disqualification of some of the interpreters of Vatican II and of a reduction of the possible interpretations of the conciliar documents."[62]

If it is true that the synod marked the beginning of a gap between different interpretations of the council, two descriptions of the rift within post–Vatican II Catholicism are worth noting and are connected with the widening gap between neo-Augustinians and neo-Thomists. The first comes from Joseph Komonchak, who gave a threefold description of Catholic positions about Vatican II between the 1980s and the 1990s. Komonchak saw a "progressive" interpretation of the council, which emphasized the rupture between pre- and postconciliar Catholicism; a "traditionalist" interpretation, which saw the rupture as a schismatic detour from the tradition of the Church; and a "mediating" position, the most important interpreter of which was Joseph Ratzinger, with his assessment of the reception of Vatican II centered on the assumption of "a contrast between an incarnational and eschatological view of the Church's relation to the world," with Ratzinger having "made clear his own preference for the latter."[63]

No less interesting is the threefold description of the debate about Vatican II given by Avery Dulles immediately following the synod. Dulles saw a "neo-Augustinian" tendency, a "communitarian school" (how Dulles referred to neo-Thomism), and a "liberationist" reception of Vatican II. The liberationist interpretation of Vatican II was rooted in the theology and episcopate of non–North Atlantic world countries (especially Africa and Latin America) and was carried by the advocates of liberation theology who desired a politically involved Church that was confrontational and militant. On the other side, the communitarian school had a humanistic outlook, convinced that great progress had been made as a result of Vatican II and that it was necessary to implement collegial and synodal structures within the Catholic Church. At present, the role of the neo-Augustinian tendency and neo-Thomist school has been decisive, while not always visible, in shaping the debate about Vatican II in the first fifty years of its reception.

In this direction, the work of David Tracy, with his distinction between analogical and dialectical imagination for Christian theology, portrays a defining feature of post–Vatican II theology in the culture of pluralism, where Christian theology builds a correlation between the two sources of Christian discourse, namely, Christian texts and common human experience and language. David Tracy's contribution to the theological debate after Vatican II casts a light on the fundamental framework of the debate on the council. While he did not participate directly in the debate about Vatican II, Tracy's major work, *The Analogical Imagination* (1981), recognized the tensions that were clearly visible in post–Vatican II Catholicism concerning the relationship between the Church and the modern world and the interpretation of *Gaudium et spes*.[64] By associating "analogical imagination" with Catholicism's embrace of metaphor, sacrament, and image, and "dialectical imagination" with the emphasis on the Protestant idea of God's inaccessibility, Tracy paraphrased the tensions within Catholic theology between neo-Thomists (analogical imagination) and neo-Augustinians (dialectical imagination).

However, it is worth remembering that, even in post–Vatican II Catholic theology, neo-Augustinians and neo-Thomists are not as conflicting and mutually excluding as they may seem: "As speculative systems, Augustinianism and Thomism are opposed to each other. Yet neither one can exclude its opposite."[65] Understanding the rift between Augustinianism and Thomism is fundamental to understanding the debate about Vatican II and the resurfacing of a "theological fault line" between the two schools. But it must be clear that this fault line originated from the outstanding event in Catholic theology of the twentieth century, that is, the surmounting of neo-Scholasticism. "It was Karl Rahner and Hans Urs von Balthasar above all who set the standard for the breakthrough in our century; and this was so even though their ways were later to part to some degree—or perhaps for that very reason."[66]

THE CLASH OF NARRATIVES

POST-SYNOD RESEARCH ON WHAT ACTUALLY HAPPENED AT VATICAN II (1985–2005)

The 1985 Synod of Bishops on Vatican II was supposed to settle the controversy on the hermeneutics of the council and impose an official set of guidelines for the reception, but these expectations were not met at all. What followed the synod was an even more vibrant intellectual effort to discover the meaning of what happened at Vatican II by way of a series of studies on the history of the council. However, more knowledge about the history of the council seems to have brought less agreement on the role of Vatican II for the Church in the twenty-first century.

As Richard John Neuhaus wrote in 1987, before his conversion to Roman Catholicism: "Something happened called Vatican II, and there is general agreement on much of what happened."[1] What was clear then was that the "general agreement" was based on a sense of belonging to the same generation of Catholic faithful and theologians more than on historical knowledge about what actually happened at the council. Until the 1980s, theological-historical scholarship about Vatican II knew little beyond the basics about the development of the individual documents, the role of the different actors (bishops, theologians), the role of the Roman Curia, and the influences of non-Catholic Churches and the world as witnesses to the debates between the council fathers. Beyond the general agreement, the tension between two parties was visible already in the 1980s, deep in the background of the theological debate. Neuhaus stated:

> When it comes to the interpretation of the Council, there is a "party of discontinuity" and a "party of continuity," the former speaking of the pre–Vatican II church and the post–Vatican II church almost as though they were two different churches, the latter affirming the continuity of the church in a manner that comes close to suggesting that not much of consequence happened at Vatican II. Each party has its own hermeneutical principles for interpreting Vatican II, and the principles are frequently employed in a way that is reminiscent of what in literary criticism is called "deconstructionism," an approach that tends to end up by denying the reality of the text.[2]

Neuhaus observed that after the 1985 Synod of Bishops, one fact had become even clearer: "In all the changing definitions of sides and alignments, the contest over the interpretation of Vatican II constitutes a critical battlefront in our society's continuing cultural wars."[3]

Visible not only in the United States but also in Europe and in Latin America from the late 1980s, this division about the hermeneutics of Vatican II called historians and theologians to engage in a new phase of research on the council. In 1987, the German theologian Hermann J. Pottmeyer pointed out the beginning of this new phase in the reception of Vatican II, given

the fundamental lack of hermeneutical principles for the interpretation and reception of the conciliar decisions. He wrote:

> Two interpretive approaches are in conflict, espe-
> cially in the second phase of reception: one looks
> exclusively to the new beginnings produced by the
> conciliar majority, the other looks exclusively to
> statements that were taken over from the prepara-
> tory schemata at the instigation of the minority and
> reflect preconciliar theology.[4]

The third phase of reception required knowledge of the "history of the text within the Council": the study of conciliar acts
and debates and of documents such as diaries, letters, and
reports that, according to Pottmeyer, "would provide the basis
for a new phase in the reception of Vatican II."[5]

After the 1987 publication of the seminal volume *The
Reception of Vatican II,*[6] the international community of scholars of
Vatican II began in 1988 to think about the need for an international, multidisciplinary, and multivolume history of the council.
Under the leadership of Giuseppe Alberigo (1926–2007), director of the Istituto per le scienze religiose di Bologna, a series of
conferences began in December 1988 that brought together historians and theologians from every continent.[7] The aim of the
project was more than just philological precision in the history of
the individual documents:

> The question that is to be answered is not simply:
> "How was the approval of the decrees of Vatican II
> reached?" but above all: "What was the actual course
> of Vatican II, and what was its significance?" But, we
> may ask, can a reliable historical reconstruction of so
> recent an event be made at such an early date? Is a

rigorous historical treatment already possible after thirty years? In 1988 an international team of historians asked itself precisely that question as it examined the feasibility of a history of Vatican II. After wide-ranging discussion the historians agreed that a history was indeed possible.[8]

A new phase in the reception of Vatican II had thus begun with a new series of studies on the historical significance of the council. Between 1988 and 1999, international conferences were held in Paris, Leuven and Louvain-la-Neuve, Houston, Lyon, Würzburg, Moscow, Bologna, and Strasbourg.[9] The proceedings of the conferences[10] built the foundations of the historical scholarship of the five-volume *History of Vatican II*;[11] the history also became possible thanks to the official *Acta* of the council published by the Vatican.[12] The work for the five-volume *History* provided the international community of scholars with new input for research on the main characters of Vatican II, on the reception of Vatican II in the local churches,[13] on council diaries and unofficial papers, and on correspondence during the council.[14]

It is not too much to say that this twenty-year phase of research on Vatican II, which began with the synod of 1985, was symbolically closed in 2005 with the new German theological commentary of the documents of Vatican II edited by Hilberath and Hünermann,[15] and with the election of the German Joseph Ratzinger as Pope Benedict XVI in April 2005. The election of the successor of John Paul II meant indeed the end of a phase of the Vatican's reception and application of the council and the beginning of a new phase. John Paul II's complex mix of "restoration of order" for the issues *ad intra* (moral theology and ecclesiology, above all) with "openness" for the issues *ad extra* (interreligious dialogue and dialogue with the Jews) was replaced by Benedict XVI's different approach of a more direct theological level. John Paul II had inaugurated a sort of Vatican II nominalism—a certain easiness in using the brand "Vatican II" for both new phenomena in the Church (like the new Catholic movements) and the theological convictions of the last pope, who had been a member of the council. This theologically complex legacy of the twenty-seven-year pontificate was over. In 2005, with the election of Benedict XVI, it became clear that a new kind of attitude toward Vatican II was taking place. The papal address of December 2005 inaugurated a new type of relationship between papal teaching and Vatican II documents, at least for Benedict XVI's pontificate.

The international scholarship about Vatican II saw that coming. From 1985 on, Rome-based pontifical universities and academic centers were absent from the constructive part of the historiographical debate about Vatican II. It should also be noted that since the Archivio Vaticano II (the archive containing the official papers of the commissions of the council) was opened to researchers in 2002, very few historians and theologians working on Vatican II have seized this opportunity to deepen and enrich their sources index and to explore the wealth of the files of the council commissions.[16] But it is also clear that the narrative of the Roman Curia about Vatican II changed significantly with the death of John Paul II and the election of Benedict XVI in April 2005.

The feeling about the dismissal of the historicity of the council and the need for a historical hermeneutic of Vatican II was strengthened between 2005 and 2007 when some public discussions brought to light a long-lasting curial dispute with the *History of Vatican II* and its director and editor Giuseppe Alberigo. Alberigo was accused of having written the history of the council, not on the basis of the final documents voted by the conciliar fathers and approved by the pope, but on the basis of an ideologically biased and "modernist" interpretation of the "spirit of Vatican II."[17]

The attacks on the *History of Vatican II* were an indirect product of the new "theological environment" brought about by Benedict XVI. After John Paul II's death, a conservative reckoning with the Bologna school appeared more and more popular inside some Italian conservative think tanks and journalistic milieus, but its ability to provide a constructive contribution to the historiography of Vatican II went no further than some harsh and biased book reviews. Nevertheless, it should be acknowledged that due to the pontificate of Benedict XVI, Vatican II has returned as an item of debate in the life of the Church. Quite a different situation has developed, though, compared to John Paul II's view of the council as expressed in his spiritual testament: "I am convinced that for a long time yet new generations will drink from the source of riches that this Council of the twentieth century has lavished on us."[18]

The multiple anniversaries of Vatican II—in 2003, the fortieth anniversary of the liturgical constitution *Sacrosanctum Concilium* and the beginning of the liturgical reform; in 2005, the fortieth anniversary of the conclusion of the council; in 2009, the fiftieth anniversary of the announcement of the council; and in 2012, the fiftieth anniversary of the opening of the council—together with the central place of Vatican II in Benedict XVI's biography as a theologian[19] have powered a rich debate in the last few years. The impact of Joseph Ratzinger–Benedict XVI on the debate, both before and after his election, and after his famous speech of December 22, 2005, has been particularly visible regarding two issues that have become the focus of theologians' attention in the last two decades: ecclesiology and liturgy.[20]

ECCLESIOLOGY: COLLEGIALITY AND *"SUBSISTIT IN"*

Ecclesiology has been, from the time of the council debates to the present, a most delicate and complex issue because it connects the theological interpretation and reception of Vatican II on one side and, on the other, the institutional development of the governance of world Catholicism in the last fifty years.

Knowledge about the ecclesiological debate at Vatican II has considerably improved in the last three decades, especially thanks to the chapters in the five-volume *History of Vatican II*, which followed the first series of exploratory and pioneering studies on the different ecclesiologies of, or components of the ecclesiology of, Vatican II.[21] Nevertheless, theologians and historians still lack a complete history of the ecclesiological debate and of the constitution *Lumen gentium*.[22] This substantial lacuna in the scholarship on the council has not stopped the debate around some of the major theological issues. The first and most delicate issue for the balance of power within post–Vatican II Catholicism is the debate on the relationship between the papacy and the bishops. In November 1964, at the end of the debate on *Lumen gentium*, Paul VI and members of the Theological Commission prepared a text, entitled *Nota explicativa praevia*, that was meant to "clarify" some aspects of the council's treatment of episcopal collegiality found in the third chapter of the constitution. In particular, *Nota explicativa praevia* made clear that the use of the term *collegium* with regard to the bishops did not mean a society of equals, and that the pope, as head of the *collegium*, could act either personally or collegially.[23] *Nota explicativa praevia* states:

> As Supreme Pastor of the Church, the Supreme Pontiff can always exercise his power at will, as his very

office demands. Though it is always in existence, the College is not as a result permanently engaged in strictly collegial activity; the Church's Tradition makes this clear. In other words, the College is not always "fully active [*in actu pleno*]"; rather, it acts as a college in the strict sense only from time to time and only with the consent of its head.[24]

The legacy of the end of the debate on *Lumen gentium* and the unexpected addition of the *Nota explicativa praevia* about the third chapter of the constitution contributed to the post–Vatican II debate, in which ecclesiologists have pointed out many substantial elements for the hermeneutic of the ecclesiology of the council, including the relationship existing between the ecclesiology of the papacy solemnly approved at Vatican I and the more collegial ecclesiology of Vatican II. Pottmeyer pointed out the necessity of integrating the two different ecclesiologies and of interpreting one in light of the other:

> Like Vatican I, Vatican II was unable to complete its work. While Vatican I was hindered by a war, Vatican II was unable to complete the reform of the Church and ecclesiology because the maximalist interpretation of Vatican I, combined with pragmatic concerns, stood in the way. The work of Vatican II has remained a building site. Alongside the old edifice of nineteenth- and twentieth-century Vatican centralization arise the four mighty supporting columns of a renewed Church and a renewed ecclesiology: the Church as people of God; the Church as sacrament of the kingdom of God in the world; the college of bishops; and ecumenism.[25]

Pottmeyer's research has also looked insightfully at the historical work of the German Jesuit historian Klaus Schatz, who proved the growth of papal primacy as a historical fact, thus advocating a more dynamic reception of the ecclesiogical change brought about by Vatican II. Schatz wrote:

> The ecclesiology of *iurisdictio*, or rather that of Vatican I, and the still older and now rediscovered ecclesiology of communio are placed side by side but remain unconnected, and this lack of connection is more serious in Church practice than in theology. The tension is exacerbated by the understandable Roman policy of permitting no weakening of Rome's own authority in face of crises in the postconciliar Church and making use of "collegiality" more or less as it seems opportune in service of more efficient direction of the Church but not permitting it to become a disturbing and critical element or a risk factor.[26]

Regarding the role of the bishops and local Churches, the Dominican ecclesiologist Hervé Legrand highlighted the underdeveloped reception of Vatican II in terms of a recognition of an intermediate ecclesiological level between the papacy and individual bishops. Such recognition would acknowledge the existence of a synodal-regional level between individual local Churches and rectify the polarized papacy-bishops reception (with no middle level) of the ecclesiology of Vatican II in the ecclesial praxis and in the 1983 Code of Canon Law. Legrand aimed to rediscover the relationship between episcopal *collegium* and the concrete expressions of the communion between the individual local Churches—expressions that were very much present in the great tradition of the Church—and to revive the regional level of Catholic governance in light of the historicity of papal primacy.[27]

In the post–Vatican II ecclesiological debate, the laity seems to have disappeared as an issue worthy of consideration. The documents of Vatican II maintained the concept of a lay apostolate next to the ideal of Catholic Action—slightly more independent of the ecclesiastical hierarchy but still in need of a "mandate" coming from it. However, in postconciliar theology, the satisfaction of the pre–Vatican II laity with the theological concessions of the council to their ecclesiological dignity has somehow contributed to a lack of interest in the issue. On the other side, the dissatisfaction of many "Vatican-II Catholics" with the narrow limits of the role of the laity as seen by John Paul II and Benedict XVI has made the issue one of advocacy more than one of detached scholarly research. Moreover, one of the new faces of post–Vatican II Catholicism has been the "volatility" of the laity: the end of the golden age of Catholic Action (with its compactness and firm obedience to the hierarchy) and the flourishing of new Catholic movements (such as Communion and Liberation, the Community of St. Egidio, Focolare, the Neocatechumenal Way, Cursillos de Cristiandad, and the Regnum Christi movement of the Legionaries of Christ) have paradoxically weakened the interest for a theology of the laity.[28]

Theologically less insightful, but still telling about recent trends in the hermeneutics of Vatican II, have been the attempts to "normalize" the ecumenical shift of Catholic ecclesiology that took place at the council. The passage *"subsistit in"* of *Lumen gentium* 8—"This Church [the Church of Christ], constituted and organized in the world as a society, subsists in the Catholic Church"—was a fundamental step in affirming that the Catholic Church and the Church of Christ were not completely coextensive: "This much debated change suggested that the church of Christ was at least in some manner to be encountered in non-Catholic Christian communities as well. This chapter was overwhelmingly approved."[29]

The attempt to reinterpret "*subsistit in*" in a way contrary to the mind of Vatican II has gained some attention in recent years.[30] The reinterpretation attempts to match that careful wording—"*subsistit in*"—first with the simple *subsists* and then with a simple *is*, thus minimizing the differences between the final document *Lumen gentium* and the document on the Church from the preparatory phase, which emphasized the juridical dimension and the identification of the Roman Church with the Mystical Body of Christ.[31] Such reinterpretation of *Lumen gentium* 8 ignores the intention of the council about this change in the language of the ecclesiological constitution. This attempt has been refuted on the basis of the history of *Lumen gentium* and of the debate on ecumenism at Vatican II,[32] and also on the basis of a comprehensive theological interpretation of the ecumenical turn of the council.[33]

Nevertheless, the interpretation that the Congregation for the Doctrine of the Faith offered for *Lumen gentium* 8 (especially between 1992 and 2000) has gained traction in the last few years among conservative Catholics. Despite the weaknesses of these attempts, this detour from the scholarly debate is crucial because it also represents a recent trend in the Vatican interpretation of the council's ecclesiology. On June 29, 2007, the Congregation for the Doctrine of the Faith issued "Responses to Some Questions Regarding Certain Aspects of the Doctrine of the Church," the focus of which was the interpretation of *Lumen gentium* 8. It affirmed, in continuity with *Communionis notio* and the declaration *Dominus Iesus* (published by the Congregation for the Doctrine of the Faith, in 1992 and 2000 respectively), that "the use of this expression [*subsistit in*], which indicates the full identity of the Church of Christ with the Catholic Church, does not change the doctrine on the Church."[34] This official interpretation of "*subsistit in*" has sparked considerable debate,[35] but not as much as expected, thanks to the crisis of Catholic ecumenism after the previous success that had been hard fought even in the Roman Curia, that is, the *Joint Declaration on the Doctrine of Justification* between Roman Catholics and Lutherans in 1999.[36]

LITURGY AND THE "REFORM OF THE REFORM"

The five-volume *History of Vatican II* edited by Giuseppe Alberigo and Joseph Komonchak provided new information about the key role of the liturgical debate within the council and about the dynamics in the preparatory and conciliar liturgical commissions.[37] Nonetheless, studies on *Sacrosanctum Concilium* published almost concurrently with the *History* focused on an ideological continuity between the early twentieth-century liturgical movement and *Sacrosanctum Concilium*, and thus they overlooked the impact of the constitution on Vatican II as such.[38]

The many studies published for the fortieth anniversary of *Sacrosanctum Concilium* in 2003 did not offer anything decisive.[39] The Tübingen-based five-volume *Herders theologischer Kommentar zum Zweiten Vatikanischen Konzil* contributed to a new appreciation of *Sacrosanctum Concilium*.[40] In the volume of *Kommentar* devoted to *Sacrosanctum Concilium* and in the *History of Vatican II*, Reiner Kaczynsky stressed the novelty of the constitution in the context of the history of the councils and of the liturgy.[41] More profoundly, he emphasized the purpose of chapter five of *Sacrosanctum Concilium*—the centrality of the paschal *mysterium*—not only as a center of the constitution but also as a "heart word" for Vatican II.[42]

Yet it seems that many commentaries on *Sacrosanctum Concilium* are outrun by the haste and aggressiveness—rather than intellectual command—of the advocates for a revision of the liturgical reform of Vatican II. In the last few years the influential calls for a "reform of the reform" of the liturgy have fueled a debate about the fortunes and misfortunes of *Sacrosanctum Concilium* and have called forth defenses of the historical memory of that postconciliar period,[43] rather than defenses of the deep theological implications and ecclesiological depth of the constitution. The debate on the council has compelled the advocates of Vatican II to defend the liturgy as reformed by the council. However, they have failed to emphasize that liturgy was not only the chronological starting point of Vatican II but also the theological starting point. Perhaps more important, the ecclesiological constitution, the first document debated and approved by the council—on November 22, 1963, with a majority vote of 2,162 to 46 after a debate featuring 328 oral interventions—was the first and most undisputed common ground of the council fathers.

Some scholars have underscored that somewhere between the nostalgia for the pre–Vatican II era and the undeniable contribution of *Sacrosanctum Concilium* to the liturgical life of the Catholic Church lies the continuity between Pius XII's encyclical *Mediator Dei* and Vatican II, and between Pius X's *motu proprio Tra le sollecitudini* (1903) and Vatican II.[44] The mix of tradition and *ressourcement* in theological discourse has generated ambiguity in the debate, which John O'Malley recently analyzed in his book *What Happened at Vatican II*.[45]

The liturgical constitution *Sacrosanctum Concilium* has been approached differently by the two hermeneutical and historiographical traditions of Vatican II—the pro-majority and the pro-minority traditions. Most pro-majority interpreters of Vatican II have looked at *Sacrosanctum Concilium* as the first reform of the council, the beginning of the event, but have seemed to entrust the defense of its profound message and implications to liturgists, who prefer the more comprehensive and ecclesiological approach based on *Lumen gentium* and the relationship between the papacy and the episcopate for the implementation of Vatican II. On the other hand, in the last decade pro-minority and essentially anticonciliar interpreters of Vatican II have surprisingly appeared to have given up the effort for a direct reinterpretation of the council and its ecclesiology, and have moved toward a downgrading of Vatican II through a dismissal of *Sacrosanctum Concilium* and a trivialization of the deep theological meaning of the liturgical reform. Despite the trivialization, some pro-minority interpreters of the council have a grasp of *Sacrosanctum Concilium* that is richer than the grasp of the average defender of Vatican II. Indeed, the definition of *Sacrosanctum Concilium* as "le parent pauvre de l'hermeneutique conciliaire" (the "forgotten element in the hermeneutics of Vatican II") is correct because, as we have seen, its hermeneutical function has been consistently downplayed.[46]

The hermeneutics of *Sacrosanctum Concilium* in the Church's life is far from purely theoretical. In the recent years' endless debate over the meaning of the constitution, it is difficult to distinguish those debaters who are aware of what is at stake from the theologians who deal with liturgical reform as just one issue among many. In this respect, the awareness of the ongoing debate on liturgy is now, fifty years after John XXIII's announcement of the council, not very different from the state of awareness of most bishops and theologians regarding this issue on the eve of Vatican II.[47] Nonetheless, the fortieth anniversary of the solemn approval of *Sacrosanctum Concilium* stirred debate about the role of liturgy in the postconciliar Church,[48] in light of a post–Vatican II period in which the implementation of the liturgical reform was the most visible example of the complexity of the relationship between the spirit and the letter of the council. More recently, Benedict XVI's *Summorum Pontificum* (July 7, 2007), his *motu proprio* concerning the liturgy, has revived interest in the destiny of *Sacrosanctum Concilium* specifically and, more generally, the role of Vatican II in the theological orientation of Benedict's pontificate.

Although it may sound peculiar, looking at the spectacular effects of *Sacrosanctum Concilium* in the Catholic Church during the last forty years places the observer before a sort of "tragic destiny" for the liturgical constitution. In the history of the hermeneutics of Vatican II, the liturgical reform seems to face a nemesis—a kind of retribution for having overlooked the connections between the liturgical constitution and the overall hermeneutics of Vatican II. This neglect was not shared by Joseph Ratzinger, whose attention to the theological and ecclesiological implications of the liturgical reform characterized some of his major works, first as a theologian and then as Roman pontiff.[49] Starting in 2005, and not only through the *motu proprio* of July 2007, the pontificate of Benedict XVI has put considerable effort into emphasizing the need for a "reform of the liturgical reform," which, especially in the English-speaking world, has caused an additional debate within the Church in the United States on the occasion of the 2009 approval by the Roman Congregation for Divine Worship and the Discipline of the Sacraments of the new English translation of the Roman Missal. The new translation, which followed *Liturgiam authenticam*—the Vatican's 2001 instruction on the translation of liturgical texts—took shape at the International Commission on English in the Liturgy (ICEL) and was seen by many liturgists as "a dead stop to the composition of new texts for the English liturgy that might have been inspiring examples of inculturation."[50]

CONFLICTING CONCILIAR NARRATIVES

The debates between deeply entrenched positions on ecclesiology and liturgy give witness to the existence of a new theological environment around Vatican II. It is indeed indisputable that the Catholic conservative narrative about Vatican II received a formidable boost by the election of Benedict XVI; nonetheless, it is true that the anti-Vatican II *revanche* mentality had already found important room for expansion during John Paul II's pontificate and in the doctrinal policy of Cardinal Ratzinger during his tenure as Prefect of the Congregation for the Doctrine of the Faith (1981–2005).[51] On the one side, during the pontificate of John Paul II, a staunch defense of the council in the name of the personal experience of the pontiff as a council father did not exclude a sometimes casual labeling of phenomena, movements, and theological insights as the "direct fruit" of Vatican II, thus endorsing a kind of Vatican II nominalism coming from John Paul II. On the other side, the doctrinal policy of Cardinal Ratzinger never disavowed a clearly conservative reading of Vatican II in the name of literalism: an interpretation of the literal texts of Vatican II aimed at countering the liberal interpretation of the council allegedly based on its pure spirit.

For many years the Vatican was the expression of a contradiction between two partially conflicting visions on the council: John Paul II's fundamentally positive view of the council and Cardinal Ratzinger's acutely pessimistic reading of the post–Vatican II period. This "dialogue" of interpretations, at the beginning under some control of the pope, gave place gradually to a more important role for Cardinal Ratzinger's views. The conclave of 2005 put an end to this dialogue between the two most important interpreters of Vatican II in the first fifty years of its reception and opened a new phase, in which Ratzinger's interpretation is no longer balanced by that of John Paul II.

All that has become evident in the theological debate, as well as in the public posture of the Holy See toward the topic of Vatican II. Already in 1997, members of the entourage of the Roman Curia, feeling more secure in the decline of John Paul II's pontificate, began expressing more vocally their prior criticism of the *History of Vatican II*.[52] This initially quiet reaction against the international, multiauthored, and respected historiographical work became gradually more visible over time, especially after 2005, but it never acquired a real scholarly standing as an alternative to the international research on Vatican II. The short-lived Center for Research on the Second Vatican Council (opened in 1998 at the Pontifical Lateran University and closed after only a few years of activity) reveals not the lack of Catholic historians' interest in the subject, but the Vatican's interest in staying out of the international scholarly debate about Vatican II.

The absence of Roman theology from the debate has been replaced by the political interpretation of Vatican II given by Curia officials and by the pope. Only a few historians active at the Vatican in Rome have taken part in this. Among the critics of the Bologna school and of the *History of Vatican II* is the party of Catholic historians who emphasize the distance between an interpretation of the council that is based on the letter of the final documents and a historiography (and theology) that assumes Vatican II as a major turning point, an event in the history of the Catholic Church.[53] According to Philippe Chenaux, professor of Church history at the Pontifical Lateran University in Rome: "This interpretation of the council as an 'event' and moment of rupture is not free from ideological presuppositions. It is clearly useful for the projects and the expectations of the ones still referring mainly to the 'spirit of Vatican II.'"[54] This opposition to the interpretation of the council as a moment of discontinuity and change in the history of Catholicism is clearly different from the Lefebvrian rejection of Vatican II as such. Nevertheless, such historical revisionism about Vatican II, Catholic ultra-traditionalism, and Lefebvrian schism have thin borders in common and essentially concur in undermining the historical fact of the universal acceptance of Vatican II by the "moral unanimity" (in Paul VI's words) of the council fathers. They are instrumental in attempting to reform the reforms made possible by Vatican II in the last fifty years: liturgical reform, ecclesiology, ecumenism, and interreligious dialogue.[55]

In this sense, a growing radicalization of positions around the council has been perceivable during the pontificate of Benedict XVI: on the one side, the anti–Vatican II sentiment typical of traditionalism coming closer and closer to the Lefebvrian narrative about the council,[56] and on the other, the radicals' disappointment with Vatican II as a failed promise.[57] In a few years the ability to articulate a nuanced and cordial debate between different schools of interpretation of Vatican II, such as that between Avery Dulles and John O'Malley in *America*, will seem lost. For example, Dulles emphasized the need for continuity *and* discontinuity in the interpretation of Vatican II:

> I find the teaching of Vatican II very solid, carefully nuanced and sufficiently flexible to meet the needs of our own time and place. The artful blending of majority and minority perspectives in the council documents should have forestalled the unilateral interpretations. There is no reason today why Vatican II should be a bone of contention among Catholics. History, of course, does not stop. Just as Vatican II made important changes reflecting new biblical

studies, the liturgical movement and the ecumenical movement, we may expect future developments in doctrine and polity. Progress must be made, but progress always depends upon an acceptance of prior achievements so that it is not necessary to begin each time from the beginning.[58]

At the same time, O'Malley highlighted the radical novelty of Vatican II in terms of *style*:

Vatican II intended to make some fundamental changes in the way the church operates and that those changes, should they be put into practice, would do much to address our current situation and give us confidence for the future. Perhaps the main reason they have not been put into practice is that the radical nature of the council has never been accepted or understood. Vatican II, for all its continuity with previous councils, was unique in many ways but nowhere more than in its call for an across-the-board change in church procedures or, better, in church *style*.[59]

The tone of the debate changed after the election of Benedict XVI, concerning both the practical reception of Vatican II by the new pope and the explicitly worded reception of the council in the teaching of the successor of John Paul II. Benedict XVI's first step toward reshaping the role of the council in his pontificate was his speech of December 2005. On December 22, 2005, the newly elected pope addressed the Roman Curia and explained his interpretation of the council by defining two opposite hermeneutical approaches to Vatican II: "Two contrary hermeneutics came face to face and quarreled with each other. One caused confusion, the other,

silently but more and more visibly, bore and is bearing fruit."[60]
The pope put on one side the conciliar hermeneutic of reform,
which presumed continuity with the tradition of the Church,
and on the other side the hermeneutic of discontinuity and
rupture. Joseph Ratzinger had explained his position in the
Ratzinger Report of 1985, in which he advocated not rupture
but continuity: "This schematism of a before and after in the
history of the Church, wholly unjustified by the documents of
Vatican II, which do nothing but reaffirm the continuity of
Catholicism, must be decidedly opposed. There is no 'pre-' or
'post-' conciliar Church."[61] Nevertheless, for Benedict XVI,
the hermeneutic of reform had clearly won the day over the
hermeneutic of discontinuity and rupture. Even so, the two
most important points of his speech to the Curia were the
rejection of the idea of a "spirit of the council," as it was misleading for the interpretation of the council, and the need to
adhere to a literal interpretation of the texts:

> The hermeneutic of discontinuity risks ending in a
> split between the pre-conciliar Church and the post-
> conciliar Church. It asserts that the texts of the
> Council as such do not yet express the true spirit of
> the Council. It claims that they are the result of com-
> promises in which, to reach unanimity, it was found
> necessary to keep and reconfirm many old things that
> are now pointless. However, the true spirit of the
> Council is not to be found in these compromises but
> instead in the impulses toward the new that are con-
> tained in the texts.
>
> These innovations alone were supposed to repre-
> sent the true spirit of the Council, and starting from
> and in conformity with them, it would be possible to
> move ahead. Precisely because the texts would only

imperfectly reflect the true spirit of the Council and its newness, it would be necessary to go courageously beyond the texts and make room for the newness in which the Council's deepest intention would be expressed, even if it were still vague.

In a word: it would be necessary not to follow the texts of the Council but its spirit. In this way, obviously, a vast margin was left open for the question on how this spirit should subsequently be defined and room was consequently made for every whim.

The nature of a Council as such is therefore basically misunderstood. In this way, it is considered as a sort of Constitutional Convention that eliminates an old constitution and creates a new one. However, the Constitutional Convention needs a mandator and then confirmation by the mandator, in other words, the people the constitution must serve. The Fathers had no such mandate and no one had ever given them one; nor could anyone have given them one because the essential constitution of the Church comes from the Lord and was given to us so that we might attain eternal life and, starting from this perspective, be able to illuminate life in time and time itself.[62]

The December 2005 speech revealed not only the sharp distinction between the pope's views of the letter and the spirit of Vatican II, but also his personal perception of the time between the council and 1968: "Forty years after the Council, we can show that the positive is far greater and livelier than it appeared to be in the turbulent years around 1968." More important, in the speech the pope also challenged one of the major acquisitions of the historiography on Vatican II, that is, that the final documents of Vatican II are "the result of compromises."[63]

Finally, Benedict XVI's point in reference to the hermeneutic of rupture, and in refusing the idea of Vatican II itself as a "constitution,"[64] revealed not only his theological views but also his acute awareness of the last chapters of the ongoing historical and theological debate about Vatican II, and his wish to declare the winner of the debate. On the other side, as Joseph Komonchak has acutely observed, the audience of Benedict XVI's message on Vatican II is also the diverse world of Catholic integrism and traditionalism: "Pope Benedict's talk on the interpretation of Vatican II could be read, then, as an effort at persuading traditionalists that a distinction is legitimately made between the level of doctrine or principle and the level of concrete application and response to situations."[65]

ONGOING RESEARCH

In the last decade, between the end of the historiographical work on the five-volume *History of Vatican II* and the fiftieth anniversary of the opening of the council, research has produced significant work toward a better understanding of what happened at Vatican II and how to receive it in the Church. After decades of studies on the council, its history, and its theology, and after the discovery of enormous archives of sources all over the world, nobody doubts any longer that "something happened" at Vatican II, but *what* happened is not so obvious. The narratives diverge, but the importance of the council for the actual state of contemporary Catholicism has become a bipartisan assumption. In the last few years, a series of different volumes and articles has stressed the importance of the memory of Vatican II for the future of the Church and the unfinished work in the reception of the council.[66]

Regarding the development of a set of hermeneutical principles, Ormond Rush has provided a significant contribution: he proposes two series of triads fundamental for the appreciation of the "history of the effects" of Vatican II. The first triad is taken from philosophical hermeneutics and is formed by "understanding, interpretation, and application." The second triad concerns communicative events and is formed by "(1) the original speaker or writer or author, (2) what is spoken or written or communicated, and (3) the addressee [the audience]." In this way, Rush proposes a "reception hermeneutics" formed by

> the original event and the original authors, the documents themselves, and the people who after the event and the documents' promulgation attempt to understand, interpret, and apply them from the context of diverse cultures and contexts down through history after the event… [Thus, there is] (1) a hermeneutics of the author, (2) a hermeneutics of the text, and (3) a hermeneutics of the receiver.[67]

The role of the receiver in the process of the theological reception of Vatican II has been recently highlighted by Gilles Routhier, who connects the individuation of the "groups-subjects of the reception of the council" with the assumption of Vatican II as an "initial moment" for the reforms of the governance of the Catholic Church in the age of Vatican II.[68] The author and director of a series of studies on the local reception of the council, Routhier stressed the concept of Vatican II as a reform council and the importance of a new phase of "regional and continental conciliarity" for the reception of the council. He also stressed the nature of Vatican II as a council opening a transition toward a new era, and the need for the post–Vatican II Church to develop a practical ecclesiology that takes into account the collegial and synodal dimension expressed in the documents of Vatican II: "We probably do not need today a [Vatican Council III], but we need to allow every level of the Catholic Church and the cultures they inhabit to give new life to the synodal life and to give new ways of expression to the conciliarity of the Church."[69]

Ladislas Orsy, professor of canon law at Georgetown University, developed a similar approach to the interpretation of Vatican II, stressing the connection between the need for an institutional translation of the *communio* in the Church and for the reception of Vatican II as "a seminal council…a new course for the Church, a course that now causes turbulences but over the centuries will become an even flow."[70] For Orsy the institutional and canonical translation of the new course of Vatican II must impact the role of the episcopal conferences, of the laity, and of canon law in the life of the Church, on the basis of the need to reform "the external structures and norms to express, to promote, and to sustain the internal bond of *communio*."[71]

Also looking at Vatican II as a reform council, Peter Hünermann, the dogmatic theologian of Tübingen, recently underlined the feature of the corpus of conciliar texts as a "constitution" for the Catholic Church:

> If one looks for an analogy along the lines of a first approach to the outline of the text of Vatican II, with the goal of characterizing the decisions of the council, what results is a certain similarity with constitutional texts as drawn up by representative constitutional assemblies. This similarity is expressed in a particular way in the texts of council Vatican II and appears in a form that is highly indirect and con-

densed as compared to the Council of Trent or Vatican I.[72]

Stressing the differences in the typology of Vatican II as a council with reference to the Council of Trent and Vatican I, Hünermann employed a comparison with the Rule of St. Benedict to outline a correct understanding of the final documents of Vatican II. The identification of Vatican II as a "constitution" surely did not mean for Hünermann placing the council texts above the Gospel: "The legitimation of a council and its authority is essentially different from that of a constitutional assembly of a modern state....For this reason the conciliar text possesses an authority essentially different from that of a constitutional text."[73] Hünermann precisely stated—in the carefully worded conclusion to his essay—a proposal to consider the texts of Vatican II as a "constitutional text for the faith":

> The corpus of texts of this council recalls a similarity with the texts of a constitution. At the same time, there are profound differences between the two beginning with the authority and specificity of the material of council texts. For this reason the text of Vatican II can be prudently defined as a "constitutional text of faith." If this preliminary idea of the text of Vatican II is valid, then what follows is a whole series of problems and questions, criticisms, and also ways of interpreting Vatican II formulated without support, since they do not conform to the literary genre of the text.[74]

In contrast, Christoph Theobald, a German-French Jesuit and professor of theology at the Centre Sèvres in Paris, has proposed a different approach centered on the specific hermeneutical value of the four constitutions of Vatican II, especially *Dei Verbum*, in a major two-volume work on the reception of Vatican II.[75] Theobald opens the first volume by saying that, despite the historiographical work done on Vatican II, the clash of the interpretations has at stake "the actual identity of the council," and that at the beginning of the twenty-first century the simple act of referring to Vatican II is already an act of reception. The hypothesis is that the constitution *Dei Verbum* must be rediscovered, after having been set aside by postconciliar theology, and must be newly appreciated together with the element of the "signs of the times" in *Gaudium et spes* and with the idea of a relationship between council and history in *Dignitatis humanae*, the Declaration on Religious Freedom. The two-volume structure is used to explain his reading of Vatican II through a twofold, horizontal-vertical dimension of the council: "the vertical or theological axis of the revelation and its reception by faith, and the horizontal or 'social' axis of the communication between Church and the components of human societies."[76] The first volume is about the vertical axis and focuses on *Dei Verbum*, *Gaudium et spes*, and *Dignitatis humanae*; the second is about the horizontal axis and focuses on *Sacrosanctum Concilium*, *Lumen gentium*, and *Ad gentes*. Theobald acknowledges the "unfinished" character of the work of Vatican II and defines the contribution of Vatican II in a hermeneutic of *recadrage* ("reframing")—thus rejecting the idea of a "simple reference to organic development" for the understanding of Vatican II.[77]

In this sense, a set of hermeneutical principles proposed in the early 1990s by Giuseppe Alberigo has become, for mainstream scholarship, a common rule for the interpretation of the council documents.[78] Thanks to the fruits of this historiographical school, very few—save those who dream of a restorationist design for the Catholic Church—question the need to also use the category of "event" to fully understand the historical and theological significance of Vatican II. Alberigo's five-volume *History of Vatican II* has become not only the standard for a complex and international history of the ecumenical council,[79] but also a symbol for the division among the narratives about Vatican II. In the early seventeenth century, Paolo Sarpi's *History of the Council of Trent* was countered by the apologetic history of Trent by Cardinal Pallavicino; now, the Bologna school's *History of Vatican II* has become the target of neo-conservative polemics in their effort to build an alternative narrative about Vatican II— but without the brilliancy and consistency of Pallavicino.[80]

In this regard, John O'Malley's *What Happened at Vatican II* received and developed the insights of the Bologna school and opened the debate on one major issue, so far underdeveloped, concerning the language of Vatican II. According to him, the council deserves and needs to be read in its intertextual character and spirit. O'Malley also tackled the conspicuous absence of serious studies on two major players—Paul VI and the so-called conciliar minority—in the historiography of Vatican II, and identified three "issues-under-the-issues," that is, the possibility of change in the Catholic Church, the relationship between center and periphery, and Vatican II as a "language event." His judgment of the outcome of the debates on all of these is sharper than the others that preceded his:

> On the final outcome of the council the minority left more than a set of fingerprints, which means that it left its mark on the three issues-under-the-issues. On the center-periphery issue the minority never really lost control. It was in that regard so successful that with the aid of Paul VI the center not only held firm and steady but, as the decades subsequent to the council have irrefutably demonstrated, emerged even stronger.[81]

6

MACRO-ISSUES OF THE DEBATE ABOUT VATICAN II

Whether the Catholic Church is moving "toward a stable narrative of Vatican II"[1] or not, the council has irreversibly penetrated the DNA of modern Catholicism. The intellectual quest for a common language among the different theological interpretations of Vatican II reflects the pastoral and ecclesial problem of whether a shared interpretation of the council in the life of the Church fifty years after its completion can exist. Thus, at the turning point of the fiftieth anniversary of the commencement of Vatican II, there is on the table a set of core hermeneutical issues crucial for the debate on Vatican II and the relationship between theology, the Catholic Church, and the role of the council in the life of the Church. The most visible issues, as they emerge from this short history of the debate on Vatican II, include (1) the understanding of Vatican II as the end of or the beginning of the renewal, (2) the view of the dynamics of the council texts in their position regarding the development of Catholic theology, and (3) the issue of change and historicity in the Church and in theology.

VATICAN II: THE END OF OR THE BEGINNING OF THE RENEWAL?

One of the major fault lines in the interpretation of Vatican II lies between the view of the council as the end and conclusion of a process of renewal based on the letter of Vatican II, and the view of the council as the beginning of a renewal based on the perception of the council as more than the collection of its final documents. This fault line mirrors the distinction between emphasizing the letter of the council documents and interpreting that letter within the Vatican II spirit, following the intention of the actors of the event and of its recipients. This version of Vatican II as either the end or the beginning reveals the practical and ecclesial implications of this hermeneutic as well as the stark difference between the two interpretations. The advocates of Vatican II as the beginning of the renewal can easily demonstrate that their augmentative view reflects what has always happened in the history of postconciliar periods—including, for Vatican II, some of the major decisions of Paul VI (who opened the path toward the official approval of the "new Catholic movements"), and in the interreligious efforts of John Paul II (who expanded the letter of the conciliar declaration *Nostra aetate* through a "magisterium of acts," for example, his meetings in Assisi in 1986 and in Damascus in 2001). On the other side, the party holding the "originalist" view of the council as the impassable boundary for the renewal of the Church sees clear limitations in the difficulty even to articulate the content of the letter of Vatican II, as if it were possible to detach it from the developments that occurred in the postconciliar magisterium.[2]

This rift sees a historical argument—a priori—in the gap between the expectations and the results of Vatican II: "Even before the council ended in 1965, there was a discrepancy between what the bishops hoped they had accomplished and what had happened."[3] However, from a theological point of view—a posteriori—if it is true that Vatican II is "a compass" for the future of the Church (as it is written in the spiritual testament of John Paul II), it is difficult to deny Vatican II the status of an epoch-making, paradigmatic event.

The perception of Vatican II as a beginning goes back to a lecture by Karl Rahner in 1965, during the last few weeks of the final session, entitled "The Council: Beginning of a Beginning."[4] Rahner developed this insight in the framework of his vision of the history of Christianity—not according to the chronology of the papacy, the relationship between Church and State, or even the history of the councils—but according to "macroperiods" in the history of Christianity. This way, Vatican II becomes not only a beacon for the future of the Church, but also a transitional moment:

> Has the Second Vatican Council a lasting significance?...The answer to our basic question may be given in the indicative, but in the last resort it is an imperative, addressed to the Church of today and tomorrow. Such an imperative implies prognoses, expectations, apprehensions, which at present can only be somewhat uncertainly conjectured. Behind our basic question lies the conviction that this Council brought to the future Church new tasks and new challenges to which reactions must still be expected.[5]

Rahner also affirmed that "the Council made a new start possible and legitimate."[6]

Rahner's view of Vatican II is original and representative of the hermeneutic that sees the council not as the end, but as the beginning of a turning point of renewal for Catholicism, an unprecedented event, similar only to the Council of

Jerusalem in chapter 15 of the Acts of the Apostles. In this interpretation, the shift made possible by Vatican II takes over the role that both Rome and Athens played in the history of Christianity—both in the history of its theological language (the Greek *logos* and the Roman *law*) and in the history of its institutional development between the Emperor Constantine and the nineteenth century (the Imperial Church and the Church as a *societas iuridice perfecta*, a "perfect community").[7]

Rahner's idea of macroperiods in the history of Christianity has been recently reshaped by Christoph Theobald in his monumental hermeneutical work about the council. Theobald wrote: "Vatican II made available, out of the circle of historians and theologians, the deep work of memory and revision of the theological tradition, and introduced this work into a collective process on 'ecumenical conversion' of mentalities—an ongoing process at every level within the Catholic Church, the Churches, and the ecclesial communities."[8]

In this sense, viewing Vatican II as a moment of the beginning of renewal places the council fully in the history of the ecumenical councils (just as Trent was only the beginning of the Tridentine era), but at the same time places it under the scope of its uniqueness. Cardinal Karl Lehmann effectively explained the distinctiveness of Vatican II in the history of the councils:

> We are used to thinking about the process of reception of a council from the starting point of a clear, measurable, and given amount of texts. With this it would be much easier to follow, establish, and categorise the process of the reception in "models." But with Vatican II it is different. Not only do we have an unprecedented amount of text and a broad range

of assertions, but also a certain amount of movement and tension moving from Vatican II.[9]

In Cardinal Lehmann's view, the element of the spirit of Vatican
II does not come from a liberal or open-ended interpretation of
the change, but from a theological dynamic: "Certainly in the
event of the council there is the breath of the Spirit of God.
There is no doubt that not every 'novelty' can be attributed
directly to the Spirit. But some groundbreaking changes have
something to do with the dynamic of renewal of the Spirit."[10]

Accepting the idea of Vatican II as the beginning often
implies accepting it as an event of the Spirit, whose impulse did
not abandon the Church after the end of the council. Conversely, seeing in Vatican II the end of the renewal assumes a
different pneumatological vision and a clearly negative assessment not only of what happened *after* the council, but also of
much of what happened *during* it. In this sense, the present
clash of narratives cannot be solved only through the study of
the history of Vatican II and of its documents, but also through
a genuine discernment of the elements of a reception pneumatology: "*sensus fidelium*, the work of theologians, and the over-
sight of the magisterium, in that order."[11]

Acknowledging the very idea of the reception of the
council means acknowledging Vatican II as the beginning of
the process of reception; playing down the theological dignity
of the reception equals identifying the letter of the documents
of Vatican II with the conclusion of the process, that is, with
its final documents—and vice versa. Reception is a theological
reality closely connected to the historical experience of the life
of the Church, not only of the councils, and not only of
Vatican II.[12] Vatican II is different because it is the first council of a Catholic "World Church." Ladislas Orsy recently
defined it as "a seminal council, probably more so than any

other in history."[13] This perspective does not imply a permanent revolution in the Church, but it assumes the theological (more than the practical) impossibility of returning to the pre–Vatican II period; it also sees in the future of the Church the unfinished agenda of the council and thus calls for a dynamic implementation of Vatican II. Walter Kasper defined the future perspective of the council listing the four theological issues it opened—but did not close: the Church as *mysterium*; the return to the sources, the Word of God, and liturgy; the implementation of communion and collegiality in the Church; and ecumenism, mission, and inculturation.[14] Looking at this agenda, it is certainly true that the last fifty years of debate about the council have worn out the debaters, but not Vatican II, the richness of which vastly exceeds the party lines of liberal versus conservatives.[15]

The dynamic of the postconciliar debate, with its tendency to establish boundaries between the different hermeneutics along political-ideological fault lines, shows that the macro-issue of the council as the end of or the beginning of the renewal is primarily ecclesiological. The majority of theologians perceive Vatican II's rediscovery of the ecclesiological dimension of *ressourcement* (in addition to and not instead of the papal primacy developed by the Tridentine era and crystallized by Vatican I) as the first step in this renewal. Interestingly, that makes the call for a Vatican Council III less likely, not more likely, as Gilles Routhier has noted:

> Probably on the agenda there is not, today, the convocation of a [Vatican Council III], but the creation of the conditions, at every level of the Catholic Church in its different cultural settings, to give new life to the synodal dimension of the Church and to remain

open to new ways of expressing the conciliarity of the Church.[16]

In this perspective, the relationship between Vatican I and Vatican II most clearly calls for an interpretation of the council that is open to the future, viewing the work of Vatican II as "a building site" in the words of Hermann Pottmeyer:

> Like Vatican I, Vatican II was unable to complete its work. The work of Vatican II has remained a building site. Alongside the old edifice of nineteenth- and twentieth-century Vatican centralization arise the four mighty supporting columns of a renewed church and a renewed ecclesiology: the church as people of God; the church as sacrament of the kingdom of God in the world; the college of bishops; and ecumenism. While the building erected by centralization awaits demolition, as the old St. Peter's Basilica did in its day, the four supporting pillars of a renewed church and a renewed ecclesiology wait to be crowned by the dome that draws them into unity.[17]

Seeing in Vatican II the end of the process equals seeing the "pastoral" character of the council, with *pastoral* being used to belittle it, in contraposition to "dogmatic" ecumenical councils. Moreover, refusing to see in Vatican II the beginning of renewal is an assertion not only unfaithful to the intention and the history of Vatican II; it also shows scant confidence in the ability of the Church to manage change on the basis of a Spirit-assisted understanding of the "signs of the times."[18] Here, the either-or of Vatican II as the end of the renewal or the beginning of the renewal is another way to describe the opposition between the conception of Catholicism as a phenomenon dominated by a culture (Greco-Roman, European, Western, and so on) or as a communion guided by the Spirit and able to transcend and enlighten every particular culture.

THE INTERTEXTUAL DYNAMIC OF THE COUNCIL DOCUMENTS

Most historians and theologians of the council have reached a mainstream consensus affirming that Vatican II is both a corpus of documents and an event, and that it should be known and understood both in its letter and in its spirit. But the recent emphasis that polemics have given to the relationship between *letter* and *spirit* implies the need for research to take a step forward from the history of the council to a history of post–Vatican II theology, that is, of the reception of Vatican II in postconciliar theology. Reckoning with Vatican II and trying to understand the actual dynamics of the interactions between its texts assumes the ability to take the step from (1) comments on the council's final texts (the first wave of research between the late 1960s and the early 1980s), to (2) the history of the composing of the texts (research between the 1980s and the latest decade), and finally to (3) the history of the texts' use in post–Vatican II theology.[19]

In this sense, the emphasis of the early postconciliar period on the ecclesiological statements of Vatican II (*Lumen gentium* and *Gaudium et spes* especially) seems to have made room now for a new balance in the approach to the corpus of the council. Between the end of Vatican II and the 1970s, the hermeneutical approach of Karl Rahner had its center of gravity in the ecclesiological shift from the *societas perfecta* to a less juridical and more sacramental view of the Church. In 1966, in the introduction to the authoritative *Commentary on the Documents of Vatican II*,

Herbert Vorgrimler described two of the most influential approaches to the documents of Vatican II. The first approach followed the December 5, 1962, speech given by Giovanni Montini (Paul VI), then cardinal archbishop of Milan, who systematized the ecclesiological issue through a twofold vision: the nature of the Church and the activity of the Church (*ecclesia ad intra* and *ecclesia ad extra*). Karl Rahner proposed the second approach, in three parts: "1. The Church's fundamental understanding of itself in the dogmatic constitution on the Church *Lumen gentium*; 2. The inner life of the Church [the documents *Sacrosanctum Concilium*, *Dei Verbum*, *Christus Dominus*, and *Apostolicam actuositatem*]; 3. The exterior commission of the Church [*Unitatis redintegratio*, *Nostra aetate*, *Ad gentes*, *Gaudium et spes*, and *Dignitatis humanae*]."[20]

In this debate in the first years of the post–Vatican II period, a particular theologian, the "Bolognese" Giuseppe Dossetti, emphasized the role of the constitution on revelation, *Dei Verbum*, and the liturgical constitution, *Sacrosanctum Concilium*, as the "hermeneutical axis of the corpus of Vatican II." This position was far from the council's mainstream interpretation of the "people of God" and from its emphasis on ecclesiology, but it was indicative of the debate around the issue in the approach to Vatican II during the first two decades.[21] The first twenty years of the post–Vatican II debate came to an end in 1985 with the first turning point in the theological history of the postconciliar period, when the Extraordinary Synod of Bishops stated: "The theological interpretation of the conciliar doctrine must consider all the documents both in themselves and in their close interrelationship, so that the integral meaning of the council's affirmations—often very complex—might be understood and expressed."[22] The synod's conclusions did not close the debate but, as it often happens, they acknowledged the work in progress and opened a door for development: it is a fact that in the last twenty-five years the theological debate has evolved toward a much more complex approach to the specificity of the final documents. The theological debate about Vatican II has accepted the idea of the literary genres of the documents and their style as expressive of the style of the whole council.[23] At the same time, it has become even clearer than before, thanks to now-available, detailed studies on the history of the most important documents of the council, that there is a need to respect both the intratextuality and the intertextuality of these texts, together with a related need to avoid separating letter and spirit.[24] So the debate about the dynamics of the council texts in their use in Catholic theology now has two different but *not* incompatible approaches to this issue.

On one side there are the advocates of a "theologal axis" in the interpretation of the corpus of Vatican II. In the interpretation of Christoph Theobald, the ecclesiological architecture of Vatican II was built around two dimensions, horizontal and vertical. The horizontal dimension of the Church (*ad intra* and *ad extra*) must be balanced with the vertical dimension by giving priority to the idea of revelation expressed in the constitution *Dei Verbum* (and in the Declaration on Religious Liberty, *Dignitatis humanae*). Theobald explained his approach to the corpus of Vatican II in his comments on the view of Vatican II itself as a "constitution" (as proposed by Peter Hünermann in 2005), and subsequently in his recent work *The Reception of Vatican II*, an impressive and comprehensive contribution to the debate on council hermeneutics. Theobald proposed a dynamic hermeneutics of conciliar texts through a crossing of horizontal (*Lumen gentium, Unitatis redintegratio, Nostra aetate, Gaudium et spes*) and vertical (*Dei Verbum, Dignitatis humanae, Lumen gentium, Sacrosanctum Concilium*) dimensions in the conciliar texts and a profound consideration of the historical nature of the texts:[25]

Is it possible to define the unity of the corpus of Vatican II without referring to the normative role of the Canon of the Scriptures? Is it possible to define this unity without showing how the corpus of Vatican II positions itself in its relationship with the Scriptures in their uniqueness—explicitly (in *Dei Verbum*) and implicitly (in the way Scriptures are quoted)—and at the same time in its relationship with the Tradition—explicitly and implicitly—that is, towards extratextual instances like the name of God and of Jesus and the work of the Holy Spirit?[26]

For Theobald, the Church is the meeting point of the horizontal and vertical dimensions of the texts of Vatican II, and the unity of Vatican II is given, not by its style or its literary genre, but by a systematic coherence in its theology around the horizontal-vertical scheme. Concerning the intertextual dynamic of the documents of Vatican II, Theobald recently called for a new role of *Dei Verbum* as the text best equipped to handle the profound issues of reform and historicity in theology and in the Church:

> *Dei Verbum* is really the great document of Vatican II that could not only articulate and unify theologically the different issues of the regulation (*dispositio*)— Scriptures, tradition, and magisterium—but [that] also tried to honor the other two phases of the hermeneutical conscience of the Church, that is, the principle of reform (particularly decisive from an ecumenical point of view) and the historicity of the cultures of the receivers of the Gospel.[27]

In this approach, centered on the pivotal role of *Dei Verbum* for the theology of Vatican II, Theobald is not alone. The American Jesuit Jared Wicks, for example, recently emphasized the derivative and not original role of the ecclesiology of the council for the understanding of the council itself:

> Some editions place *Lumen gentium* at the head of the Vatican II constitutions, but would not the conciliar ecclesiology be better contextualized if it were placed *after* the council text starting with "hearing the word of God reverently and proclaiming it confidently..." and ending with "the word of God... stands forever," as does *Dei Verbum*?[28]

The role of *Dei Verbum* is directly connected to the issue of the hermeneutics of Vatican II as a whole; a correct hermeneutical approach to the texts of Vatican II applies both the idea of *ressourcement* and the need to respect the hierarchy of truths in theology—two principles of a Catholic theology re-rooted in the Word of God via *Dei Verbum*.[29] In this sense, Ormond Rush's hermeneutics of the council documents must be remembered, which distinguish between the hermeneutics of the authors, of the texts, and of the receivers. Rush has given a nuanced view of the central role of *Dei Verbum* in the context of the other documents:

> According to the principle of the hierarchy of truths, *Dei Verbum* has a certain priority over the others, since one's notion of church (*Lumen gentium*), its worship (*Sacrosanctum Concilium*), and its relationship to the world (*Gaudium et spes*) should derive from the prior notion of how one conceives God's revelation and its reception-transmission in history....*Dei Verbum*,

therefore, although promulgating teaching regarding a "higher" doctrine according to the hierarchy of truths, must be interpreted (re-interpreted) in the light of the other documents.[30]

A second approach to the corpus of Vatican II as a source for theology is more focused on the central role of the documents in their historical making, in their literary genre, and in their style. This alternate approach does not see in *Dei Verbum* the first step in the hermeneutics of Vatican II, given the intertextual dimension of every theological issue handled by the council, but favors a multilateral and intertextual approach to the council documents for the theological understanding of every issue. On this perspective, John O'Malley has emphasized in the last few years—not only in *What Happened at Vatican II*, but also thanks to his studies in *Four Cultures of the West*[31]—the need to understand the specificity of the genre and of the style of the documents of Vatican II in order to grasp their theological value and to overcome the entrenching of the conservative/reactionary and progressive/liberal positions. For O'Malley, the hermeneutics of Vatican II should pay more attention to new areas such as the council's language, as well as inter-documental history and other inter-documental issues. The acknowledgment of the specificity of the texts shows the invitational style of Vatican II: the fact that Vatican II was a "language event" needs to be taken seriously by its interpreters "in constructing a hermeneutic for interpreting the council."[32] For O'Malley, acknowledging the style of Vatican II makes it possible to recognize the spirit of the council as an expression of fundamental orientations that cut across the council documents, even while being based firmly on them—and also makes it possible to recover the spirit of the council through an intertextual and intratextual approach.

With a similar approach, Gilles Routhier explained his view of the council documents in reference to the issue of style, affirming that proclaiming one document of Vatican II as primary could lead to a misunderstanding of the intertextual meaning of the council:

> The renewed attention that we see today towards the hermeneutics of the documents of Vatican II is promising and dangerous at the same time. It is promising because, now that the experience of Vatican II becomes a distant memory, we have what the council left us with, that is, the texts. But this going back to the texts is dangerous if it is an excuse to make of the documents of Vatican II a stack of individual statements, autonomous from their literary context, independent from the act of their enunciation, detached from their background, truncated from the tradition that carries them, and independent from their style, so that these individual statements could be set in opposition one to the other.[33]

Peter Hünermann has developed a similar analysis in a long and audaciously reasoned essay that underlines the feature of the *corpus* of conciliar texts as a constitution for the Catholic Church: the intertextual dynamic of the documents does not see the preeminence of a particular document or issue precisely because the council itself as a whole is a "text" to be interpreted:

> The legitimation of a council and its authority is essentially different from that of a constitutional assembly of a modern state....For this reason the conciliar text possesses an authority essentially dif-

ferent from that of a constitutional text....[Never-theless,] the corpus of texts of this council recalls a similarity with the texts of a constitution. At the same time, there are profound differences between the two, beginning with the authority and speci-ficity of the material of council texts. For this reason the texts of Vatican II can be prudently defined a "constitutional text of faith."[34]

This constitutional character of the texts of Vatican II can be seen in their hermeneutical and ecclesial consequences:

The question now is how to transmit the knowledge of this corpus of texts of Vatican II to the people of God, to the different groups and states in the Church. It is not enough if only students of theology, future priests, seminarians, and pastoral ministers learn these texts. What we need at all levels of the life of the Church is an ongoing dialogue, an ongoing discussion and a reflection about this corpus.[35]

These two different hermeneutical approaches—the theo-logal axis around *Dei Verbum*, and the emphasis on Vatican II as a corpus defined by its style—share much and are not necessar-ily opposed to one another because both presuppose and assume the historicization of Vatican II and the hermeneutical shift pro-duced by the historical studies on the council. The Italian theo-logian Giuseppe Ruggieri called for a varied hermeneutic of Vatican II, viewing in the theologal axis proposed by Theobald an attitude that is respectful of the historical dimension of the documents of Vatican II. There is indeed a consensus among theologians about a hermeneutical approach to the council texts that takes into account the history of those documents and their literary forms and genre, thus comparing and differentiating between the hermeneutic of the council documents and the hermeneutic of the texts affirmed by *Dei Verbum* for the Bible:

> In the debate taking place now nobody is challenging the need to interpret in a coherent and organic way the different documents approved by the council. But once we enunciate the principle of the unity of the corpus of Vatican II, we see time and again the difficulties concerning the biblical canon, with a fundamental difference, that is, the corpus of Vatican II does not enjoy divine inspiration like the Bible.[36]

CHANGE AND HISTORICITY IN THE CHURCH AND IN THEOLOGY

The very first years of the post–Vatican II Church were marked by the crisis of papal authority on the basis of the teaching on birth control contained in Paul VI's 1968 encyclical *Humanae vitae*. Not just a concern for moral theologians or Catholic married couples, this crisis explained one of the crucial issues of Vatican II, that is, how to manage change and continuity in the Catholic Church: "The crisis engaged how the church deals with the past, in this instance with past papal pronouncements."[37] In a way, the history of the debate about *Humanae vitae* explains why that landmark papal teaching of 1968 inaugurated the disillusionment of the post–Vatican II era, and symbolized the beginning of a fracture between the magisterium and a theology that had left metaphysics as its center of orientation and increasingly become a theology of "salvation history," where human history also becomes a real source for theological work.

The relevance granted by theologians to history as *locus theologicus*, that is, the role of history and change in theology, is by far the most important factor in the parting ways of Catholic theology after Vatican II and about Vatican II.[38] On one side, there are those who see in the "hermeneutic of continuity" (later, in Benedict XVI's speech of 2005, in more nuanced and quickly forgotten words, the "hermeneutic of reform") the only possible hermeneutical option regarding Vatican II, that is, the need to interpret Vatican II in continuity with the previous tradition, especially Trent and Vatican I. On the other side, there are those who see in Catholicism a period *before* Vatican II and a period *after* Vatican II, and that there is a clear "discontinuity" and change between these two periods, Vatican II representing the turning point for this discontinuity and change, which is, in their view, clearly for the better.

Joseph Komonchak is correct in his assessment that "the traditionalist interpretation of Vatican II makes use of a similar distinction between pre- and postconciliar Catholicism but reverses the appreciation."[39] Nevertheless, it is also true that the traditionalist interpretation of Vatican II exemplifies the extreme version of the same discomfort of the "moderate traditional" (as opposed to the extreme traditionalist) mind-set about the new historical awareness of Catholic theology. They seem to ignore that the alleged "flight from eternity"[40] is not a discovery of Vatican II, and even less a product of the historical and theological studies on what happened (and did *not* happen) at Vatican II.

In the contemporary debate about the council it has become clear that the issue of change is not mainly related to the hermeneutical relationship between Vatican I and Vatican II, but to the relationship between Trent and Vatican II. In this respect, it is remarkable to see how particular this chronological interpretation of "continuity" is as it attempts to establish a steady but clearly selective continuity in the last five centuries of the history of the Church. This "continuist" interpretation does not accept the idea of any historical discontinuity occurring between the Constantine era and the Imperial Church in the first millennium, and the Council of Trent and the Tridentine era in the second, and between Trent and the twentieth century. This interpretation of the relationship between historicity in the Church and theology on one side, and the issue of continuity/reform/discontinuity on the other side, often forgets a basic fact about the obvious amount of discontinuity in the history of the councils. To give an example dear to the traditionalist mind-set, it is known that Trent meant a significant change from the "lack of clarity" of the previous theological tradition.[41] It is also known that the success of the Council of Trent in creating what we now call the Tridentine era was the result of the discontinuities between the letter of the decrees of the council and the application of those decrees, that is, the council's "spirit," in the post-Trent Church.[42] On the other hand, Komonchak argues that there is both continuity and discontinuity at Vatican II in relation to Trent: "There is no point at which Vatican II departs from any dogmatic teaching of the Council of Trent, but at Vatican II, Trent and its problematic ceased to serve as the supreme touchstone of faith. The tradition was no longer read in the light of Trent; Trent was read in the light of the tradition."[43]

It is now clear that the appeal to the spirit of Vatican II did not always give birth to extravagant applications in the life of the postconciliar Church, as we can see from the case of the "new Catholic movements."[44] In light of Church history it becomes clear that the supposed opposition between the *letter* of the texts of an ecumenical council and its *spirit* cannot be solved easily with a simple contraposition of the two hermeneutical moments in favor of the pure spirit, nor by affirming an ancillary role of the spirit versus the letter. In 1966, Joseph Ratzinger was expressing a common appreciation of Vatican II, when he wrote about the council: "It was undoubtedly a rupture, but a rupture within a fundamentally common intention."[45] In this sense, we should reconsider, more than twenty-five years later, what Cardinal Ratzinger said in 1985 about the state of the debate about the council: "I believe that the true time of Vatican II has not yet come, that its authentic reception has not yet begun: its documents were quickly buried under a pile of superficial or frankly inexact publications. The reading of the *letter* of the documents will enable us to discover their true *spirit*."[46]

It is now also clear that in the scholarship about Vatican II we are well past the stage of the "superficial or frankly inexact publications," if we grant some credibility to the historical and theological broad consensus about the historiographical work done on the council at least in the past two decades. The question is whether the advocates of continuity are ready to accept—as they have already done explicitly or implicitly for the Council of Trent or for Vatican I—the historical fact of discontinuity and change between the precouncil period and the council itself, and the inevitable gap between the intentions and the letter of the texts of the council and the "unintended consequences" (in John O'Malley's words) of the postcouncil period.[47]

If it is true that, in the post–Vatican II period, Catholic theology has sometimes indulged in the "para-council" and forgotten the real council, this is certainly true on both sides of the aisle. On one side, the impatient exaltation of discontinuity and renewal has been matched on the other side by the self-deluding illusion of the possibility of a perfect linearity between pre–Vatican II theology, the texts of the preparatory phase of Vatican II, and the final texts. It is time to re-acknowledge that the character of Vatican II as an event is a fundamental aspect of the history of this council, as it was for every council: but the hermeneutical framework (the way the modern mind approaches a text) has changed.[48] For Vatican II, the feature of "event" has been more dramatic and the change more visible, thanks to the global dimension of the council, the first of post-European Catholicism.[49] But Vatican II is also part of the history of the councils: to deny the measure of change within Vatican II is to deny the character of Vatican II as an event and of the previous ecumenical councils. The important role of events in Church history is a factor, an element of continuity, and truly part of the genius of Catholicism: assuming a perfect continuity between Vatican II and the previous tradition would put Vatican II in the category of the exceptions from the history of the councils of the Church.[50]

The debate about the relationship between the letter and the spirit, between continuity and discontinuity, does not promise much because this issue is not typical of Vatican II. What is typical of Vatican II is the dimension of the relationship between the Church and the modern world, the assumption of history in its epistemological value for Catholic theology, and the fact that Vatican II is not a paradigm in itself (as it is, for example, in Hans Küng's view of Vatican II as the "ecumenical postmodern theological paradigm"),[51] but a "paradigmatic example" of the complex relationship between continuity and discontinuity.[52]

A correct hermeneutical approach to the issue of continuity/discontinuity calls for a non-originalist reception of Vatican II. Giuseppe Alberigo acknowledged the gap between the expectations of Vatican II and its conclusions: "It seems that Vatican II, even though burdened by a number of decrees of preconciliar inspiration, did on the whole go beyond the expectations and bring about a deeper and more organic 'turnabout' than the petitions voiced on the eve of the Council had the farsightedness and courage to desire."[53] According to Alberigo, and to many other interpreters of the council, this gap is typical of Vatican II, which arrived too early for the globalization of the Church, in comparison with Trent, which arrived too late in reaction to Martin Luther and the reformers. This distance between the expectations and the results of the council seems, in this kind of interpretation, to have been absorbed by the dynamics of Vatican II and the energies that it unleashed for the transition to a new age of Catholicism.

In this view, the relationship between Vatican II and the history of Catholicism is not only one that identifies a turning point around the council, but also one that offers a more dramatic view, centered more on the event and open to the self-healing ability of the Church to absorb rifts and fault lines—and ultimately to change.[54]

Epilogue

For nonspecialists, a book on the history of the debate about Vatican II could seem like a kind of meta-narrative destined to narrow the field even more. But the intent of this book is to show that Vatican II was a paradigmatic event of the new era in the history of the Catholic Church: not only for what happened *at* Vatican II but also for what happened *after* Vatican II as well. Following the introductory chapter, each chapter represented a step in the history of the debate about Vatican II; the reader will judge how far we have progressed from chapter 2 through 6.

What will happen *to* Vatican II in the future? Will the council face a silent abrogation of its work? This is not beyond the interest of this author, but it is beyond the scope of this book.

In the 1980s especially, interpreters of the council applied to Vatican II the idea of a paradigm shift, the definition given during the years of the council by Thomas S. Kuhn in *The Structure of Scientific Revolutions*.[1] But to understand the comparison between the history of science and the history of theology, one of the most important laws has been referred to much less: a major scientific advance is almost always overestimated in the short run for its consequences, and underestimated in the long run. Fifty years after the event of Vatican II, we find ourselves in that crucial moment of passage between the short run and the long run: the clash of narratives about Vatican II encounters here the perennial law of the reception of the councils of the Church. Giuseppe Alberigo, recalling the worrisome memorandum sent between 1600 and 1612 by Robert Bellarmine to Pope Clement VIII on the progress of the reforms decided by the Council of Trent (between 1545 and 1563), estimated that it took at least fifty years for the beginning of the reception of Trent.[2]

John O'Malley's "law of unintended consequences" explains this passage from the immediate postcouncil period to the view of Vatican II for world Catholicism in the long term. The current underestimation of Vatican II in many circles is no different from the underestimation of the consequences of the discovery of vaccines against smallpox and polio. What is disturbing, especially in the last few years, is that younger generations of Catholics have been credited by theological pundits with a detached or even skeptical view of Vatican II that symbolizes polarization, culture wars, and division in the Church— something these younger generations allegedly feel the need to take distance from, as if the common ground they seek could only be a ground as distant as possible from Vatican II. My experience teaching Vatican II could not be more different from this misperception. Whether liberal or conservative, Catholics and Catholic students of every theological and spiritual orientation know well that longing for and aspiring to revive the period before Vatican II is a dream nourished only by people who do not live the real, day-to-day reality of the Church. Ecumenism, religious freedom, and the rejection of anti-Semitism cannot be reduced to partisan issues: the post–9/11 world has revealed the prophetic value of documents like *Nostra aetate*, whose theological necessity had vastly outgrown the narrow boundaries of its short text. To belittle Vatican II is to belittle these achievements as well, and disparaging these achievements means disparaging the very theology of Vatican II that brought about not only this opening of the Church *ad extra*, but also the reflection of the Church *ad intra*.

Epilogue

The election of Pope Benedict XVI in 2005 and the reopening of the debate about Vatican II are two "signs of the times" for the Church of the early twenty-first century, which represent for the Church simultaneously a time of progress and regress. For Catholics, the council is not a foil in their self-identification of the ways of being Catholic, but a real reference and a given condition of existence, especially for Catholicism outside the geopolitical and cultural boundaries of the North Atlantic hemisphere. Richard John Neuhaus's 1987 statement about Vatican II—"The contest over the interpretations of Vatican II constitutes a critical battlefront in our society's continuing cultural wars"[3]—must also be read in reverse: the substantial and undeniable ability of the Catholic Church to remain together in the Western hemisphere and in the rest of the world despite these wars (cultural and otherwise) owes much to Vatican II and its interpretations. Behind the very identity of the Church and its relationship with the modern world there is a specific (if sometimes unconscious or indirect) interpretation of Vatican II. That is why a history of the debate about Vatican II is the consequential next step after the completion of the *History of Vatican II*.

In the first decades of the post–Vatican II period, the debate on the council lived through major moments of discussion and dispute.[4] The 1970s saw the beginning of the entrenching of different positions along a fault line in the interpretation of Vatican II within Catholic theology; the seventies also saw the birth of a schismatic group (the Lefebvrians) whose existence found motivation only in their rejection of Vatican II and in particular new orientations of the Church *ad extra*. The Code of Canon Law of 1983 and the final results of the Extraordinary Synod of Bishops of 1985 steered the hermeneutics of Vatican II toward a more cautious interpretation of the relationship between *letter* and *spirit* of the council and inaugurated the complex reception of Vatican II by John Paul II. Coming just a few months after the election of John Paul II's successor, Benedict XVI's speech of December 22, 2005, conveyed a clear message about the much-anticipated shift in the doctrinal policy about Vatican II from the former cardinal prefect of the Congregation for the Doctrine of Faith: that speech celebrated the passage of Joseph Ratzinger's take on Vatican II from the level of an individual theologian, if not a powerful cardinal, to the level of the Roman pontiff's official interpretation of the council.

The everlasting political and institutional constraints of the "office of Peter" have clearly shown Benedict XVI the difficulty of turning back from the language and orientation of Vatican II: not for the first time in history, the unintended consequences of a major historical event have had an effect outside the boundaries of the institution as well. Thus, an external framework for the interpretation of Vatican II has been created that is not less visible and tangible than the hermeneutical balance struck by the Church as a whole—popes, bishops, clergy, monks, theologians, families, lay men and women, pastoral ministers, and missionaries. The debate about interpretation undoubtedly feels the ongoing pressure that was initially invited by Vatican II itself—from its council opening, *Gaudet Mater Ecclesia*, delivered on October 11, 1962, to *Gaudium et spes*, the Pastoral Constitution on the Church in the Modern World, promulgated on December 7, 1965, the day the council ended.

As an example of this pressure, consider the "incident" of January 2009 when, one day after Benedict XVI's decision to lift the excommunication of the Lefebvrian bishops of the Priestly Fraternity of St. Pius X, one of those bishops publically denied the Holocaust in a widely seen TV interview. Global reaction to the interview revealed how profoundly the culture of Vatican II has penetrated the modern world, which is now begging the Church to be faithful to those teachings *ad extra.*[5]

The complexity of the debate has also to do with the fact that the history of the post–Vatican II Church intertwines with the growth in knowledge and awareness of Catholic theology about Vatican II. It is a remarkable fact that during the first decades of the debate about Vatican II, the historical and theological research on the ecumenical council has acquired information and developed approaches to the "thing"—Vatican II—that were only imaginable in the 1970s or 1980s. Scholars of very different theological affiliations now know much more about Vatican II, both in its day-by-day unfolding and in its overall and epoch-making dimension: as an event of Church history, of the history of theology, of the history of ideas, and of political and social history. The Catholic Church now knows a significant amount of information about Vatican II, from different cultural approaches and geographical points of view. The amount of information about the change that happened at Vatican II is probably more than Catholic theology expected, and maybe more than the Church as an institution was ready to handle. But the communion of the Church is much better equipped to handle the rediscovery of its past than, for example, the intellectuals on the payroll of the Communist party of the Soviet Union, who when faced with the permanent, ideological manipulation of recent history were mocked with this popular Soviet-era joke: "We know exactly what the future will be. Our problem is with the past: that keeps changing."

However, the "Catholic past" has not been changed by the lively historical and theological debate about Vatican II— a comforting sign of the vitality of the Church in a world where the so-called neo-atheism takes pride in seeing faith and debate as opposite terms. The historicization of Vatican II starting in the late 1980s has clearly introduced a hermeneutical shift in the theology of Vatican II. Therefore, it is not surprising that the abundance of information about Vatican II has not solved the issue of the need for a coherent and shared interpretation of the council documents. We may have the impression sometimes that knowing more about Vatican II has complicated the issue of its interpretation, but choosing to know less about the council is not a viable option. It's not even possible anymore.

NOTES

CHAPTER 1

1. See Benedict XVI, Christmas Address to the Roman Curia, December 22, 2005, in *Insegnamenti di Benedetto XVI*, vol. 1 (2005) (Vatican City: Libreria Editrice Vaticana, 2006), 1018–32, and at http://www.vatican.va/holy_father/benedict_xvi/speeches/2005/december/documents/hf_ben_xvi_spe_20051222_roman-curia_en.html.

2. See Gilles Routhier, "Recherches et publications récentes autour de Vatican II," *Laval Théologique et philosophique* 56 (2000): 543–83; 58 (2002): 177–203; 60/3 (2004): 561–77; Massimo Faggioli, "Concilio Vaticano II: bollettino bibliografico (2000–2002)," *Cristianesimo nella Storia* 24/2 (2003): 335–60; Massimo Faggioli, "Concilio Vaticano II: bollettino bibliografico (2002–2005)," *Cristianesimo nella Storia* 26/3 (2005): 743–67; Massimo Faggioli, "Vatican Council II: Bibliographical Overview 2005–2007," *Cristianesimo nella Storia* 29/2 (2008): 567–610; Jared Wicks, "New Light on Vatican Council II," *Catholic Historical Review* 92 (2006): 609–28; Wicks, "Further Light on Vatican Council II," *The Catholic Historical Review* 95 (2009): 546–69.

3. It is also true that publications on Vatican II have always been successful for publishers, as we can see from the history of the most popular collection of conciliar documents, *Kleines Konzilskompendium*, edited by Karl Rahner and Herbert Vorgrimler (Freiburg: Herder, 1966), which celebrated its thirty-fifth edition in 2008 (Freiburg: Herder, 2008).

4. See the suggested readings at the end of this volume for some examples of the many diaries and journals kept by bishops and theologians at Vatican II. For a list of published and unpublished

diaries and journals, see Massimo Faggioli and Giovanni Turbanti, *Il concilio inedito: Fonti del Vaticano II* (Bologna: Il Mulino, 2001).

5. Giuseppe Alberigo, "For a Christian Ecumenical Council," in *Toward Vatican III: The Work That Needs to Be Done*, ed. David Tracy, with Hans Küng and Johann B. Metz (Nijmegen, Netherlands: Concilium; New York: Seabury Press, 1978), 57–66, quotation at 57.

6. John W. O'Malley, *What Happened at Vatican II* (Cambridge, MA: Belknap Press, 2008), 311.

7. For the first studies on the language of the final documents of Vatican II see *Indices verborum et locutionum Decretorum Concilii Vaticani II*, 11 vols. (Bologna: Istituto per le scienze religiose, 1968–86); Philippe Delhaye, Michel Gueret, and Paul Tombeur, eds., *Concilium Vaticanum II. Concordance, Index, Listes de fréquence, Tables comparatives* (Louvain, 1974).

8. See Joseph Komonchak, "Augustine, Aquinas, or the Gospel *sine glossa*? Divisions over *Gaudium et spes*," in *Unfinished Journey: The Church 40 Years after Vatican II*, ed. John Wilkins (London: Continuum, 2004), 102–8. It is worth noting that Karl Rahner agreed with Ratzinger that the first part of *Gaudium et spes* was too optimistic.

9. Hans Urs von Balthasar, "Communio—A Program," *Communio* 1 (1972): 3–12, quotation at 3.

10. The original text of the homily in Italian is at http://www.vatican.va/holy_father/paul_vi/homilies/1972/documents/hf_p-vi_hom_19720629_it.html. The English translation is quoted from Nicholas Lash, *Theology for Pilgrims* (Notre Dame, IN: University of Notre Dame Press, 2008), 259.

11. See Marcel Lefebvre, *I Accuse the Council!* (Kansas City, MO: Angelus Press, 2007; original French: *J'accuse le Concile!* Paris: Éditions Saint-Gabriel, 1976).

12. See Tracy, *Toward Vatican III*; Alberto Melloni, "Breve guida ai giudizi sul concilio," in *Chi ha paura del Vaticano II?* ed. Alberto Melloni and Giuseppe Ruggieri (Rome: Carocci, 2009), 107–45.

13. See Karol Wojtyla (Pope John Paul II), *Sources of Renewal: The Implementation of the Second Vatican Council*, trans. P. S. Falla (San Francisco: Harper & Row, 1980. Original Polish: *U podstaw odnowy. Studium o realizacji Vaticanum II* (Krakow: PTT, 1972).

14. See Eugenio Corecco, "Aspects of the Reception of Vatican II in the Code of Canon Law," in *The Reception of Vatican II*, ed. Giuseppe Alberigo, Jean-Pierre Jossua, and Joseph Komonchak (Washington, DC: Catholic University of America Press, 1985), 249–96.

15. *The Final Report of the 1985 Extraordinary Synod* (Washington, DC: National Conference of Catholic Bishops, 1986), I.2 and I.3.

16. Ibid., I.5.

17. Ibid.

18. See John W. O'Malley, *Tradition and Transition: Historical Perspectives on Vatican II* (Wilmington, DE: M. Glazier, 1989).

19. *Final Report*, I.5

20. Joseph Cardinal Ratzinger (with Vittorio Messori), *The Ratzinger Report: An Exclusive Interview on the State of the Church*, translated by Salvator Attanasio and Graham Harrison (San Francisco: Ignatius Press, 1985).

21. See Alberic Stacpoole, ed., *Vatican II Revisited: By Those Who Were There* (Minneapolis, MN: Winston Press, 1986); Giuseppe Alberigo, Jean-Pierre Jossua, and Joseph A. Komonchak, eds., *The Reception of Vatican II* (Washington, DC: Catholic University of America Press, 1987); Norbert Greinacher and Hans Küng, eds., *Katholische Kirche, wohin? Wider den Verrat am Konzil* (Munich: Piper, 1986); Timothy E. O'Connell, ed., *Vatican II and Its Documents: An American Reappraisal* (Wilmington, DE: Michael Glazier, 1986); René Latourelle, ed., *Vatican II: Assessment and Perspectives: Twenty-five Years After (1962–1987)*, 3 vols. (New York/Mahwah, NJ: Paulist Press, 1988–89); Lucien Richard, with Daniel T. Harrington and John W. O'Malley, eds., *Vatican II, The Unfinished Agenda: A Look to the Future* (New York/Mahwah, NJ: Paulist Press, 1987).

22. *History of Vatican II*, 5 vols., ed. Giuseppe Alberigo; English version, ed. Joseph A. Komonchak (Louvain: Peeters, 1995–2006; Maryknoll, NY: Orbis, 1995–2006).

23. The official documents of the governing bodies of Vatican II (commissions, plenary assemblies) and of the participants were published in *Acta et documenta Concilio Oecumenico Vaticano II apparando.* *Series I—Antepraeparatoria* (Vatican City: Typis Polyglottis Vaticanis, 1960–61); *Series II—Praeparatoria* (Vatican City: Typis Polyglottis

Vaticanis, 1964–94); *Acta Synodalia Sacrosancti Concilii Oecumenici Vaticani II* (Vatican City: Typis Polyglottis Vaticanis, 1970–99).

24. *Das Zweite Vatikanische Konzil. Konstitutionen, Dekrete und Erklärungen lateinisch und deutsch Kommentare* (Lexikon für Theologie und Kirche), 3 vols. (Freiburg: Herder, 1966–68); English version: *Commentary on the Documents of Vatican II*, 5 vols., ed. Herbert Vorgrimler, trans. Lalit Adolphus, Kevin Smyth, and Richard Strachan (London: Burns & Oates; New York: Herder & Herder, 1967–69).

25. See Giuseppe Alberigo and Franca Magistretti, *Constitutionis dogmaticae Lumen Gentium Synopsis Historica* (Bologna: Istituto per le scienze religiose, 1975); Antonio Acerbi, *Due ecclesiologie: ecclesiologia giuridica ed ecclesiologia di comunione nella "Lumen gentium"* (Bologna: Edizioni Dehoniane, 1975).

26. Rock Caporale, *Vatican II: Last of the Councils*, foreword by John J. Wright (Baltimore: Helicon, 1964); Giuseppe Caprile, *Il Concilio Vaticano II*, 5 vols. (Rome: Civiltà Cattolica, 1966–68); Yves Congar, *Vatican II. Le concile au jour le jour*, 4 vols. (Paris: Cerf, 1963–66); Henri Fesquet, *Le journal du Concile* (Forcalquier: Morel, 1966); René Laurentin, *L'Enjeu du Concile* (Paris: Seuil, 1962) and *Bilan du Concile Vatican II* (Paris: Seuil, 1967); René Rouquette, *La fin d'une chrétienté. Chroniques*, 2 vols. (Paris: Cerf, 1968); Antoine Wenger, *Vatican II*, 4 vols. (Paris: Centurion, 1963–66); Ralph Wiltgen, *The Rhine Flows into the Tiber* (New York: Hawthorn Books, 1967; Rockford, IL: Tan Books, 1985). Also see Xavier Rynne, *Letters from Vatican City: Vatican Council II (First Session): Background and Debates* (New York: Farrar, Straus & Giroux, 1963); *The Second Session* (New York: Farrar, Straus & Giroux, 1964); *The Third Session* (New York: Farrar, Straus & Giroux, 1965); *The Fourth Session* (New York: Farrar, Straus & Giroux, 1966). For a revised version of Rynne's earlier books covering all four sessions of Vatican Council II, see *Vatican Council II* (Maryknoll, NY: Orbis, 1999).

27. For syntheses, see René Aubert, *The Church in a Secularised Society* (New York: Paulist Press; London: Darton, Longman and Todd, 1978); and Otto Hermann Pesch, *Das Zweite Vatikanische Konzil, 1962–1965: Vorgeschichte, Verlauf, Ergebnisse, Nachgeschichte* (Würzburg: Echter, 1993).

28. See *Le Deuxième concile du Vatican (1959–1965)* (Rome: Ecole Française de Rome, 1989); Elmar Klinger and Klaus Wittstadt, eds., *Glaube im Prozess: Christsein nach dem II. Vatikanum: Für Karl Rahner* (Freiburg: Herder, 1984); René Latourelle, ed., *Vatican II: Assessment and Perspectives: Twenty-five Years After (1962–1987)* (New York/Mahwah, NJ: Paulist Press, 1988–89); Wolfgang Weiss, ed., *Zeugnis und Dialog: die Katholische Kirche in der neuzeitlichen Welt und das II. Vatikanische Konzil* (Würzburg: Echter, 1996).

29. See Massimo Faggioli and Giovanni Turbanti, *Il concilio inedito: fonti del Vaticano II* (Bologna: Il Mulino, 2001).

30. See Joseph Famerée, "Vers un histoire du Concile Vatican II," *Revue d'Histoire Ecclesiastique* 89 (1994): 638–41; Alois Greiler, "Ein Internationales Forschungsprojekt zur Geschichte des Zweitens Vatikanums," in *Zeugnis und Dialog*, 571–78.

31. See Giuseppe Alberigo, "Criteri ermeneutici per una storia del Vaticano II," in *Il Vaticano II fra attese e celebrazione*, ed. Giuseppe Alberigo (Bologna: Il Mulino, 1995), 12–23; now in Giuseppe Alberigo, *Transizione epocale. Studi sul concilio Vaticano II* (Bologna: Il Mulino, 2009), 29–45.

32. For some of these other titles, especially in the collections "Testi e ricerche di scienze religiose dell'Istituto per le scienze religiose di Bologna" and "Instrumenta theologica Bibliotheek van de Faculteit Godgeleerdheid" in Louvain (Belgium), see Massimo Faggioli, "Concilio Vaticano II: bollettino bibliografico (2000–2002)," *Cristianesimo nella Storia* 24/2 (2003): 335–60; Massimo Faggioli, "Concilio Vaticano II: bollettino bibliografico (2002–2005)," *Cristianesimo nella Storia* 26/3 (2005): 743–67; "Council Vatican II: Bibliographical Overview 2005–2007," *Cristianesimo nella Storia* 29/2 (2008): 567–610.

33. See José Oscar Beozzo, ed., *Cristianismo e iglesias de America Latina et vísperas del Vaticano II* (San José, Costa Rica: Cehila, 1992); also see Beozzo, *A Igreja do Brasil no Concílio Vaticano II, 1959–1965* (São Paulo: Paulinas; Rio de Janeiro, RJ: Educam, 2005).

34. See Franz-Xaver Kaufmann and Arnold Zingerle, eds., *Vatikanum II und Modernisierung. Historische, theologische und soziologische Perspektiven* (Paderborn: Schöningh, 1996); Peter Hünermann,

ed., *Das II. Vatikanum. Christlicher Glaube im Horizont globaler Modernisierung: Einleitungsfragen* (Paderborn: Schöningh, 1998); Claus Arnold and Hubert Wolf, eds., *Die deutschsprachigen Länder und das II. Vatikanum* (Paderborn: Schöningh, 2000).

35. For example, see Joseph A. Komonchak, "Vatican II as Ecumenical Council," *Commonweal*, November 22, 2002. Also see the debate between Dulles and O'Malley that appeared in *America*: Avery Dulles, "Vatican II: The Myth and the Reality," 7–11, and John W. O'Malley, "The Style of Vatican II," 12–15, both in *America*, February 24, 2003; also Dulles, "Vatican II: Substantive Teaching," 14–17, and O'Malley, "Vatican II: Official Norms," 1114, both in *America*, March 31, 2003.

36. See, for example, Ormond Rush, *Still Interpreting Vatican II: Some Hermeneutical Principles* (New York/Mahwah, NJ: Paulist Press, 2004), and the series of articles published between 2001 and 2005 by Jeffrey J. Murphy in *The Australasian Catholic Record*.

37. *Zweite Vatikanische Konzil, Dokumente und Kommentare*, ed. Heinrich Suso Brechter (Freiburg: Herder, 1966–68); English edition published as *Commentary on the Documents of Vatican II*, ed. Herbert Vorgrimler, trans. by Lalit Adolphus, Kevin Smyth, and Richard Strachan (London: Burns & Oates; New York: Herder & Herder, 1967–69).

38. Peter Hünermann and Bernd Jochen Hilberath, eds., *Herders theologischer Kommentar zum Zweiten Vatikanischen Konzil*, 5 vols. (Freiburg: Herder, 2004–6); Peter Hünermann, ed., *Das Zweite Vatikanische Konzil und die Zeichen der Zeit heute* (Freiburg: Herder, 2006).

39. See Francis A. Sullivan, "Response to Karl Becker, SJ, on the Meaning of Subsistit in," *Theological Studies* 67/2 (June 2006): 395–409; Francis A. Sullivan, "Quaestio disputata. The Meaning of *Subsistit in* as explained by the Congregation for the Doctrine of Faith," *Theological Studies* 69/1 (2008): 116–24.

40. See Christoph Theobald, ed., *Vatican II sous le regard des historiens* (Paris: Médiasèvres, 2006); Raymond F. Bulman and Frederick J. Parrella, eds., *From Trent to Vatican II: Historical and Theological Investigations* (Oxford–New York: Oxford University Press, 2006);

David G. Schultenover, ed., *Vatican II: Did Anything Happen?* (New York–London: Continuum, 2007); and John W. O'Malley, *What Happened at Vatican II* (Cambridge, MA: Belknap Press, 2008). For a reductionist interpretation of the council, see Matthew L. Lamb and Matthew Levering, eds., *Vatican II: Renewal within Tradition* (Oxford–New York: Oxford University Press, 2008).

CHAPTER 2

1. Joseph Komonchak, "Interpreting the Council," in *Being Right: Conservative Catholics in America*, ed. Mary Jo Weaver and R. Scott Appleby (Bloomington: Indiana University Press, 1995), 17–36, with quotation at 21.

2. See *L'avvenire della chiesa* (Brussells, 1970). *Il libro del congresso* (Brescia: Queriniana, 1970).

3. See Leo Jozef Suenens' interview, *Informations Catholiques Internationales*, May 15, 1969; José de Broucker, *The Suenens Dossier: The Case for Collegiality* (Notre Dame, IN: Fides Publishers, 1970).

4. Yves Congar, "Les lendemains de conciles," *Documents-épiscopat*, May 10, 1975, republished in Yves Congar, *Le Concile de Vatican II* (Paris: Beauchesne, 1984), 99–107, quotation at 107.

5. Theodore M. Hesburgh, "Letter of Invitation," in *Toward Vatican III: The Work That Needs to Be Done*, ed. David Tracy, with Hans Küng and Johann B. Metz (Nijmegen: Concilium; New York: Seabury Press, 1978), 3.

6. Hans Küng, "Vatican III: Problems and Opportunities for the Future," in *Toward Vatican III*, 68–69.

7. Giuseppe Alberigo, "For a Christian Ecumenical Council," in *Toward Vatican III*, 57–66, quotation at 58–59.

8. Jacques Maritain, *Le Paysan de la Garonne. Un vieux laic s'interroge à propos du temps présent* (Paris: Desclée De Brouwer, 1966); in English as *The Peasant of the Garonne: An Old Layman Questions Himself about the Present Time*, trans. Michael Cuddihy and Elizabeth Hughes (New York: Holt, Rinehart and Winston, 1968).

9. See Gerard Philips, "Deux tendances dans la théologie contemporaine," *Nouvelle Revue Théologique* 85 (1963): 225–38; Philippe Levillain, *La mécanique politique de Vatican II: la majorité et l'unanimité dans un concile* (Paris: Beauchesne, 1975).

10. See *History of Vatican II*, 5 vols., ed. by Giuseppe Alberigo; English version, ed. Joseph A. Komonchak (Louvain: Peeters, 1995–2006; Maryknoll, NY: Orbis, 1995–2006).

11. See Nicla Buonasorte, *Tra Roma e Lefebvre: il tradizionalismo cattolico italiano e il Concilio Vaticano II* (Rome: Studium, 2003); Luc Perrin, "Il 'Coetus Internationalis Patrum' e la minoranza conciliare," in *L'evento e le decisioni. Studi sulle dinamiche del concilio Vaticano II*, ed. Maria Teresa Fattori and Alberto Melloni (Bologna: Il Mulino, 1997), 173–87.

12. Ralph M. Wiltgen, *The Rhine Flows into the Tiber: A History of Vatican II* (Rockford, IL: Tan Books, 1985; first edition, New York: Hawthorn Books, 1967), 1. Wiltgen's book serves as Kenneth D. Whitehead's basic source for his book, *The Renewed Church: The Second Vatican Council's Enduring Teaching about the Church* (Ave Maria, FL: Sapientia Press, 2009).

13. Romano Amerio, *Iota Unum: A Study of Change in the Catholic Church in the Twentieth Century*, trans. John P. Parson from the second Italian edition (Kansas City, MO: Sarto House, 1996), 99. The first Italian edition was Milano: R. Ricciardi, 1985; 3rd ed., 1989. The French edition was Paris: Nouvelles editions latines, 1987. *Iota Unum* was republished in Italy in 2009 by two different publishers: by Lindau, in Turin, ed. Enrico Maria Radaelli, preface by Cardinal Dario Castrillon Hoyos, and by Fede e Cultura, in Verona. In the United States, the work of Romano Amerio was published by Angelus Press, the voice of Marcel Lefebvre's "Society of St. Pius X." Another example of this Catholic ultraconservative mind-set leaning toward Lefebvre is Roberto De Mattei's *Il Concilio Vaticano II. Una storia mai scritta* (Turin: Lindau, 2010).

14. Amerio, *Iota Unum*, 720–21.

15. For an example of such a mind-set, see Dominique Bourmaud, *Cent ans de modernisme. Généalogie du concile Vatican II* (Etampes: Clovis, 2003); in English as *One Hundred Years of Modernism: A History of Modernism, Aristotle to the Second Vatican Council*, trans.

Brian Sudlow and Anne Marie Temple (Kansas City, MO: Angelus Press, 2006).

16. See Wigand Siebel, *Katholisch oder konziliar. Die Krise der Kirche heute* (Munich; Vienna: Langen-Müller, 1978). Also see the periodicals *Iesus Christus* (for Latin America), *Convictions* (North America), *La pensée catholique, Fideliter* (France), *Mitteilungsblatt* (Germany), and *Cristianità* and *Sì sì no no* (Italy).

17. Daniele Menozzi, "Opposition to the Council," in *The Reception of Vatican II*, ed. Giuseppe Alberigo, Jean-Pierre Jossua, and Joseph A. Komonchak (Washington, DC: Catholic University of America Press, 1987), 325–48, quotation at 326.

18. See Émile Poulat, *Une église ébranlée: changement, conflit et continuité de Pie XII à Jean-Paul II* (Tournai: Casterman, 1980); Nicolas Senèze, *La crise intégriste: vingt ans après le schisme de Mgr Lefebvre* (Paris: Bayard, 2008). On January 21, 2009, Pope Benedict XVI remitted the excommunication of the bishops of the Society of St. Pius X. For the reactions against Benedict XVI's decision, see, among others, Peter Hünermann, ed., *Exkommunication oder Kommunikation? Der Weg der Kirche nach dem II. Vatikanum* (Freiburg: Herder, 2009).

19. See *History of Vatican II*, vol. 1, *Announcing and Preparing Vatican Council II Toward a New Era in Catholicism*, ed. Joseph A. Komonchak (Maryknoll, NY: Orbis, 1996), 126–31; John O'Malley, *What Happened at Vatican II* (Cambridge, MA: Belknap Press, 2008), 110–11.

20. See *History of Vatican II*, vol. 4, *Church as Communion: Third Period and Intersession, September 1964–November 1964*, ed. Komonchak (2004); O'Malley, *What Happened at Vatican II*, 244–45.

21. Together with Monsignor Lefebvre, it is also worth noting ultraconservative Bishop Geraldo de Proença Sigaud (Diamantina, Brazil) and Bishop Antonio de Castro Mayer (Campos, Brazil), supporter of the far-right movement "Tradition, Family, Property". See the homepage of the Society of St. Pius X, http://www.sspx.org.

22. See Marcel Lefebvre, *Un éveque parle: écrits et allocutions* (Morin: Paris, 1974–76); in English as *A Bishop Speaks: Writings and Addresses 1963–1976* (Edinburgh: Scottish Una Voce, 1979; 2nd American ed., Kansas City, MO: Angelus Press, 2007), 9.

23. Marcel Lefebvre, *J'accuse le concile!* (Paris: Éditions Saint-Gabriel, 1976), 9; in English as *I Accuse the Council!* (Dickinson, TX: Angelus Press, 1982; Kansas City, MO: Angelus Press, 1998).

24. Marcel Lefebvre, *J'accuse le concile!*, 20. Also see Silvia Scatena, *La fatica della libertà. L'elaborazione della dichiarazione Dignitatis humanae sulla libertà religiosa del Vaticano II* (Bologna: Il Mulino, 2004); Stephen B. Bevans and Jeffrey Gros, *Evangelization and Religious Freedom: Ad Gentes, Dignitatis Humanae* (New York, Mahwah, NJ: Paulist Press, 2009).

25. Marcel Lefebvre, *An Open Letter to Confused Catholics* (Herefordshire, UK: Fowler Wright, 1986), 105; original French, *Lettre ouverte aux catholiques perplexes* (Paris: Albin Michel, 1985).

26. The overestimation of the role of the liturgy in Lefebvre's rejection of the council has been exploited for the call for a "reform of the liturgical reform." See John Baldovin, *Reforming the Liturgy: A Response to the Critics* (Collegeville, MN: Liturgical Press, 2008).

27. Lefebvre, *An Open Letter to Confused Catholics*, 109–10.

28. Ibid., 111.

29. Ibid., 117.

30. Ibid., 118.

31. Daniele Menozzi, "Opposition to the Council," in *The Reception of Vatican II*, 325–48, quotation at 341.

32. See Denis Pelletier, *La crise catholique. Religion, société, politique en France 1965–1978* (Paris: Payot, 2002); Daniela Saresella, *Dal Concilio alla contestazione. Riviste cattoliche negli anni del cambiamento, 1958–1968* (Brescia: Morcelliana, 2005); Massimo Faggioli, *Breve storia dei movimenti cattolici* (Rome: Carocci, 2008); Gerd-Rainer Horn, *Western European Liberation Theology 1924–1959: The First Wave* (Oxford–New York: Oxford University Press, 2008); and Gerd-Rainer Horn, *The Spirit of '68: Rebellion in Western Europe and North America, 1956–1976* (Oxford–New York: Oxford University Press, 2008).

33. See O'Malley, *What Happened at Vatican II*, 311.

34. See Thomas J. Reese, *Inside the Vatican: The Politics and Organization of the Catholic Church* (Cambridge, MA: Harvard University Press, 1996).

35. See Christopher Bellitto, *Renewing Christianity: A History of Church Reform from Day One to Vatican II* (New York/Mahwah, NJ: Paulist Press, 2001). See also Giuseppe Alberigo, "Councils and Reform: Challenging Misconceptions," in *The Church, the Councils, and Reform: The Legacy of the Fifteenth Century*, ed. Gerald Christianson, Thomas M. Izbicki, and Christopher M. Bellitto (Washington, DC: Catholic University of America Press, 2008), 271–90.

36. Giuseppe Alberigo, "The Conclusion of the Council and the Initial Reception," in *History of Vatican II*, vol. 5, *The Council and the Transition: The Fourth Period and the End of the Council (September 1965–December 1965)*, ed. Komonchak (2005), 541–71, quotation at 556.

37. See Andrea Riccardi, *Il potere del papa da Pio XII a Giovanni Paolo II* (Rome-Bari: Laterza, 1993), 289–311.

CHAPTER 3

1. Edmund Schlink, *After the Council*, trans. Herbert J. A. Bouman (Philadelphia: Fortress Press, 1968); original German, *Nach dem Konzil* (Munich and Hamburg: Siebenstern, 1966). For Karl Rahner's definition, see "The Council: A New Beginning," in *The Church after the Council*, trans. Davis C. Herron and Rodelinde Albrecht (New York: Herder and Herder, 1966), 20; original German, *Das Konzil: Ein neuer Beginn* (Freiburg: Herder, 1966).

2. Among the major world Christian churches, only the Baptist World Alliance did not respond to the invitation from Rome.

3. John O'Malley, *What Happened at Vatican II* (Cambridge, MA: Belknap Press, 2008), 33.

4. André Birmelè, "Le Concile Vatican II vu par les observateurs des autres traditions chrétiennes," in *Volti di fine concilio: Studi di storia e teologia sulla conclusione del Vaticano II*, ed. Joseph Dorè and Alberto Melloni (Bologna: Il Mulino, 2000), 225–64, quotation at 230; also, Mauro Velati, "Gli osservatori del Consiglio Ecumenico delle Chiese al Vaticano II," in *L'evento e le decisioni. Studi sulle dinamiche del concilio Vaticano II*, ed. Maria Teresa Fattori and Alberto Melloni (Bologna: Il Mulino, 1997), 189–257.

5. See, for example, the Danish Lutheran Kristen E. Skydsgaard, "Le mystère de l'Église," in *Le dialogue est ouvert: Les trois premières sessions du Concile Vatican II*, ed. Oscar Cullmann (Neuchâtel: Delachaux & Niestlé, 1965), 147–71.

6. See Olivier Clément, "Vers un dialogue avec le catholicisme," *Contacts* 14 (1965): 16–37, esp. 37; and Karl Barth, "Thoughts on the Second Vatican Council," in *Ad Limina Apostolorum: An Appraisal of Vatican II*, trans. Keith R. Crim (Richmond, VA: John Knox Press, 1968), 70. George Lindbeck provides a more critical position in "Liturgy: Summit and Source," in Lindbeck, *The Future of Roman Catholic Theology: Vatican II—Catalyst for Change* (Philadelphia: Fortress, 1970), 51–75.

7. See Ulrich Valeske, *Hierarchia Veritatum: Theologiegeschichtliche Hintergründe und mögliche Konsequenzen eines Hinweises im Ökumenismusdekret des II. Vatikanischen Konzils zum zwischenkirchlichen Gespräch* (Munich: Claudius, 1968).

8. Kristen E. Skydsgaard, "The Council and Evangelical Christians," in *The Papal Council and the Gospel: Protestant Theologians Evaluate the Coming Vatican Council*, ed. Kristen E. Skydsgaard (Minneapolis: Augsburg, 1961), 139–69, quotation at 152.

9. John Moorman, qtd. in Lukas Vischer, "The Council as an Event in the Ecumenical Movement," in *History of Vatican II*, vol. 5, *The Council and the Transition: The Fourth Period and the End of the Council, September 1965–December 1965*, ed. Joseph A. Komonchak (Maryknoll, NY: Orbis, 2005), 485–539, quotation at 516.

10. John Moorman, *Vatican II Observed: An Anglican Impression of Vatican II* (London: Catholic Book Club, 1967), 184–85.

11. See Christoph Theobald, "The Church under the Word of God," in *History of Vatican II*, vol. 5, *The Council and the Transition*, 354–55.

12. Schlink, *After the Council*, 46–47.

13. Ibid., 189.

14. Ibid., 186–87.

15. Ibid., 212.

16. Oscar Cullmann, "Was bedeutet das Zweite Vatikanische Konzil für uns Protestanten?" in *Was bedeutet das Zweite Vatikanische Konzil für uns?* ed. Werner Schatz (Basel: F. Reinhardt, 1966), 20.

17. Ibid., 19.

18. Ibid., 17. For more by Oscar Cullmann, see also *Vatican Council II: The New Direction*, essays selected and arranged by James D. Hester (New York: Harper & Row, 1968).

19. See *Karl Barth in prospettiva ecumenica: Annuario di filosofia e teologia* 16/2009, special issue (Brescia: Morcelliana, 2009).

20. Barth, "Thoughts on the Second Vatican Council," *Ad Limina Apostolorum*, 68.

21. Ibid., 72–73.

22. Ibid., 77.

23. From Lindbeck's memorandum to the WCC (Spring 1964), quoted in Vischer, "The Council as an Event in the Ecumenical Movement," in *History of Vatican II*, vol. 5, *The Council and the Transition*, 485–539, quotation at 510.

24. George Lindbeck, *The Future of Roman Catholic Theology*, 3–4.

25. George Lindbeck, "Vatican II and Protestant Self-Understanding," in *Vatican II: Open Questions and New Horizons*, ed. Gerald M. Fagin (Wilmington, DE: Michael Glazier, 1984), 60.

26. Olivier Clément, "L'Église Orthodoxe et le Seconde Concile du Vatican," *Contacts* 15 (1963): 62–65, quotation at 64.

27. Clément, "Vers un dialogue avec le Catholicisme," *Contacts* 14 (1965): 16–37.

28. Nikos Nissiotis, "Was bedeutet das Zweite Vatikanische Konzil für uns Orthodoxe," in *Was bedeutet das Zweite Vatikanische Konzil für uns?* ed. Werner Schatz (Basel: F. Reinhardt, 1966), 157–88, quotation at 171.

29. The words of Lutheran minister Richard John Neuhaus, who had not yet converted to Roman Catholicism (which he did in 1990). "The Councils Called Vatican II," in Richard John Neuhaus, *The Catholic Moment: The Paradox of the Church in the Postmodern World* (San Francisco: Harper and Row, 1987), 66.

30. Karl Rahner and Edward Schillebeeckx, "General Introduction," *Concilium* 1/1 (1965): 3–4.

31. See Hans Küng, *The Church*, trans. Ray and Rosaleen Ockenden (New York: Sheed and Ward, 1968; original German *Die Kirche*, Freiburg: Herder, 1967).

32. See *A New Catechism: Catholic Faith for Adults*, trans. Kevin Smyth (London: Burns & Oates; New York: Herder and Herder, 1967).

33. See Hadewych Snijdewind, "Genèse et organisation de la revue internationale de théologie Concilium," *Cristianesimo nella Storia* 21 (2000): 645–73; Étienne Fouilloux, "I teologi cattolici dal pre al postconcilio," in *Tutto è grazia. In omaggio a Giuseppe Ruggieri*, ed. Alberto Melloni (Milan: Jaca Book, 2010), 201–15.

34. Richard Gaillardetz, *The Church in the Making* (New York/Mahwah, NJ: Paulist Press, 2006), 92.

35. Hans Urs von Balthasar, "*Communio*—A Programme," *International Catholic Review* 1 (January-February, 1972), 3–12, quotation at 3. This journal was the forerunner to *Communio: International Catholic Review*.

36. For Ratzinger's contribution to the journal *Communio*, see *Joseph Ratzinger in Communio*, vol. 1, "The Unity of the Church," ed. David L. Schindler (Grand Rapids, MI: Eerdmans, 2010).

37. Silvia Scatena, *In populo pauperum: La chiesa latinoamericana dal concilio a Medellín (1962–1968)* (Bologna: Il Mulino, 2008).

38. Gustavo Gutiérrez, "The Church and the Poor: A Latin American Perspective," in *The Reception of Vatican II*, ed. Giuseppe Alberigo, Jean-Pierre Jossua, Joseph A. Komonchak (Washington, DC: Catholic University of America Press, 1987), 193.

39. See José Oscar Beozzo, "Medellín: Inspiration et Racines," in *Volti di fine concilio*, 361–94.

40. Jon Sobrino, *The True Church and the Poor*, trans. Matthew J. O'Connell (Maryknoll, NY: Orbis, 1984), 240; original Spanish, *Santander: Sal Terrae* (1981).

41 Ibid., 242.

42. Leonardo Boff, *Ecclesiogenesis: The Base Communities Reinvent the Church*, trans. Robert R. Barr (Maryknoll, NY: Orbis, 1986), 68; original Portuguese, *Petrópolis: Vozes* (1977).

43. See Rosino Gibellini, *La teologia del XX secolo* (Brescia: Queriniana, 1992), 372–73, and *The Liberation Theology Debate*, trans. John Bowden (Maryknoll, NY: Orbis, 1987).

44. See *Theology in the Americas*, ed. Sergio Torres and John Eagleson (Maryknoll, NY: Orbis, 1976).

45. See Carmel McEnroy, *Guests in Their Own House: The Women of Vatican II* (New York: Crossroad, 1996).

46. Gertrud Heinzelmann, *Wir schweigen nicht länger! Frauen äussern sich zum II. Vatikanischen Konzil* (Zürich: Interfeminas-Verlag, 1965).

47. For Baum's theological assessment of Catholic theology after Vatican II, see Gregory Baum, *Amazing Church: A Catholic Theologian Remembers a Half-Century of Change* (Ottawa: Novalis; Maryknoll, NY: Orbis, 2005).

48. Elizabeth Schlüsser Fiorenza, "Introduction: Feminist Liberation Theology as Critical Sophialogy," in *The Power of Naming: A Concilium Reader in Feminist Liberation Theology*, ed. Elizabeth Schlüsser Fiorenza (Maryknoll, NY: Orbis; London: SCM Press, 1996), xiv.

49. Gary Dorrien, *The Making of American Liberal Theology: Crisis, Irony, and Postmodernity 1950–2005* (Louisville, KY: Westminster John Knox, 2006), 431–32.

50. Elizabeth A. Johnson, *She Who Is: The Mystery of God in Feminist Theological Discourse* (New York: Crossroad, 1992), 79.

51. See Serena Noceti, "Un caso serio della recezione conciliare: donne e teologia," *Ricerche Teologiche* XIII/1 (2002): 211–24.

52. Harriet A. Luckman, "Vatican II and the Role of Women," in *Vatican II Forty Years Later*, ed. William Madges (Maryknoll, NY: Orbis, 2005), 78–99, quotation at 93.

53. For the Canadian reception of Vatican II, see *Vatican II: Experiences Canadiennes/Canadian Experiences*, ed. Michael Attridge, Catherine E. Clifford, and Gilles Routhier (Ottawa: Les Presses de l'Universitè d'Ottawa–University of Ottawa Press, 2011). Also see Gilles Routhier, *La réception d'un concile* (Paris: Cerf, 1993); and Routhier, *Vatican II. Herméneutique et reception* (Montreal: Fides, 2006).

54. See Philip Jenkins, *The Next Christendom: The Coming of Global Christianity* (New York: Oxford University Press, 2007).

55. For the contribution of the African bishops, see Jean-Paul Messina, *Evêques africains au concile Vatican II (1959–1965)* (Paris: Karthala, 2000).

56. See *Fundamental Theology: Doing Theology in New Places*, ed. Jean-Pierre Jossua and Johann Baptist Metz (New York: Seabury Press 1979; Issue 115, 5/1978, of the journal *Concilium*); *Le Déplacement de la theologie*, ed. Jacques Audinet et al. (Paris: Beauchesne, 1977).

57. See *D'un synode africain à l'autre: Réception synodale et perspectives d'avenir, Église et société en Afrique*, ed. Joseph Ndi-Okalla and Antoine Ntalou (Paris: Karthala, 2007).

58. Adrian Hastings, *African Catholicism: Essays in Discovery* (London: SCM; Philadelphia: Trinity Press, 1989), 128–29.

59. See Éloi Messi Metogo, "Bible and Liturgy," in *African Christianities*, ed. Éloi Messi Metogo (*Concilium* 2006/4) (London: SCM Press, 2006), 56–61. See also Henriette Danette and Éloi Messi Metogo, "Le devenir de la théologie catholique en Afrique francophone depuis Vatican II," and Elochukwu Eugene Uzukwu, "Le devenir de la théologie catholique en Afrique anglophone depuis Vatican," *Transversalités* 68 (1998): 91–118 and 61–90.

60. Meinrad P. Hebga, *Émancipation d'Églises sous tutelle. Essai sur l'ère post-missionnaire* (Paris: Présence africaine, 1976); see also Gwinyai H. Muzorewa, *The Origins and Development of African Theology* (Maryknoll, NY: Orbis, 1985).

61. See Paul Pulikkan, *Indian Church at Vatican II: A Historico-Theological Study of the Indian Participation in the Second Vatican Council* (Trichur, Kerala: Marymatha Publications, 2001).

62. Peter Phan, "'Reception' or 'Subversion' of Vatican II by the Asian Churches? A New Way of Being Church in Asia," in *Vatican II Forty Years Later*, 26–54, quotation at 32.

63. Peter Phan, "Reception of Vatican II in Asia: Historical and Theological Analysis," *Gregorianum* 83 (2002): 269–85, quotation at 276; now also in Peter C. Phan, *In Our Own Tongues: Perspectives from Asia on Mission and Inculturation* (Maryknoll, NY: Orbis, 2003), 201–14.

64. Peter Phan, "Reception of Vatican II in Asia," 281.

65. See Michael Amaladoss, "Mission in Asia: A Reflection on Ecclesia in Asia," and Peter C. Phan, "Ecclesia in Asia: Challenges for

Asian Christianity," in *The Asian Synod: Texts and Commentaries*, ed. Peter C. Phan (Maryknoll, NY: Orbis, 2002), 222–35 and 249–61.

66. See Raimundo Panikkar, *The Unknown Christ of Hinduism: Towards an Ecumenical Christophany* (London: Darton, Longman & Todd, 1981); Tissa Balasuriya, *Planetary Theology* (Maryknoll, NY: Orbis, 1984); Felix A. Machado, "Le developpement de la théologie de Vatican II à nos jours: Un point de vue sud-asiatique," *Transversalités* 68 (1998): 29–59.

67. See *For All the Peoples of Asia: Federation of Asian Bishops' Conferences, Documents from 1970 to 1991*, vol. 1, ed. Gaudencio Rosales and C. G. Arévalo (Maryknoll, NY: Orbis; Quezon City, Philippines: Claretian Publications, 1992), 70.

68. See the series of articles published by Jeff J. Murphy about the Australian bishops at Vatican II in *The Australasian Catholic Record*, starting in 2001, especially "The Far Milieu Called Home: Australian Bishops at Vatican II (The Final Session: 1965)," *The Australasian Catholic Record* 80/3 (July 2003): 343–69; Richard Lennan, "Receiving Vatican II: The Australian Experience," *Journal of the Australian Catholic Historical Society*, vol. 26, 2005, 7–14.

69. As it is evident in the work of Tracey Rowland, *Culture and the Thomist Tradition after Vatican II* (London: Routledge, 2003). See Patrick O'Farrell, *The Catholic Church and Community: An Australian History*, 3rd rev. ed. (Sydney: UNSW Press, 1995). For the contribution of two notable Australian theologians to the global debate about Vatican II, see Ormond Rush, *Still Interpreting Vatican II: Some Hermeneutical Principles* (New York/Mahwah, NJ: Paulist Press, 2004), and Gerald O'Collins, *Living Vatican II: The 21st Council for the 21st Century* (New York/Mahwah, NJ: Paulist Press, 2006).

CHAPTER 4

1. On this divide see Walter Kasper, "On the Church: A Friendly Reply to Cardinal Ratzinger," *America*, April 23–30, 2001, 8–14; originally published in *Stimmen der Zeit* 12 (December 2000): 795–804. For Joseph Ratzinger's reactions, see "The Local Church

and the Universal Church: A Response to Walter Kasper," *America*, November 19, 2001, 7–11; originally published in *Stimmen der Zeit* (December 2000) and "Die grosse Gottesidee 'Kirche' ist keine Schwärmerei," *Frankfurter Allgemeine Zeitung*, December 22, 2000. The debate had started with Joseph Ratzinger, "L'ecclesiologia della costituzione Lumen Gentium," in *Il Concilio Vaticano II: recezione e attualità alla luce del giubileo*, ed. Rino Fisichella (Cinisello B.: San Paolo, 2000), 66–81. A synthesis of the debate is in Kilian McDonnell, "The Ratzinger/Kasper Debate: The Universal Church and Local Churches," *Theological Studies* 63 (June 2002): 227–50.

2. Gérard Philips, "Deux tendances dans la théologie contemporaine," *Nouvelle Revue Théologique* 85 (1963): 225–38, quotation at 225.

3. Ibid., 235.

4. See Joseph A. Komonchak, "Augustine, Aquinas, or the Gospel *sine glossa?*" in *Unfinished Journey: The Church 40 Years after Vatican II: Essays for John Wilkins*, ed. by Austin Ivereigh (New York: Continuum, 2005), 102–18.

5. Ormond Rush, *Still Interpreting Vatican II: Some Hermeneutical Principles* (New York/Mahwah, NJ: Paulist Press, 2004), 15.

6. Avery Dulles, "The Reception of Vatican II at the Extraordinary Synod of 1985," in *The Reception of Vatican II*, ed. Giuseppe Alberigo, Jean-Pierre Jossua, and Joseph A. Komonchak (Washington, DC: Catholic University of America Press, 1987), 353.

7. Hans Urs von Balthasar, *Razing the Bastions: On the Church in This Age*, foreword by Christoph Schonborn, trans. Brian McNeil (San Francisco: Ignatius, 1993; *Schleifung der Bastionen*, Einsiedeln: Johannes Verlag, 1952).

8. Hans Urs von Balthasar, *My Work: In Retrospect* (San Francisco: Ignatius, 1993; *Durchblicke*, Einsiedeln: Johannes, 1990), 51. The article was originally published with the title "Rechenschaft" in *Communio* 2 (1975): 197–220.

9. Ibid.

10. Ibid., 53.

11. Hans Urs von Balthasar, *The Office of Peter and the Structure of the Church*, trans. Andrée Emery (San Francisco: Ignatius, 1986), 176; *Der antirömische Affekt* (Freiburg: Herder, 1974).

12. Henri de Lubac, *Carnets du Concile*, 2 vols. (Paris: Cerf, 2007).

13. Henri de Lubac, *Augustinisme et théologie moderne*, Oeuvres complètes XIII (Paris: Cerf, 2008), xxiv; *Augustinianism and Modern Theology*, ed. Lancelot Sheppard (New York: Crossroad, 2000).

14. Henri de Lubac, *A Brief Catechesis on Nature and Grace*, trans. Richard Arnandez (San Francisco: Ignatius, 1984), 235; *Petite catéchèse sur nature et grâce* (Paris: Fayard, 1980).

15. Henri de Lubac, *Entretien Autour de Vatican II: Souvenirs et Réflexions* (Paris: Cerf, 1985), 76.

16. See Henri de Lubac, *Carnets du Concile* and Giuseppe Ruggieri, "Delusioni alla fine del concilio. Qualche atteggiamento nell'ambiente cattolico francese," in *Volti di fine Concilio. Studi di storia e teologia sulla conclusione del Vaticano II*, ed. Joseph Doré and Alberto Melloni (Bologna: Il Mulino, 2000), 193–224.

17. See Hansjürgen Verweyen, *Joseph Ratzinger–Benedikt XVI. Die Entwicklung seines Denkens* (Darmstadt: Wissenschaftliche Buchgesellschaft, 2007), 20–21 and 114–15.

18. See Jared Wicks, "Six Texts by Prof. Joseph Ratzinger as *peritus* before and during Vatican Council II," *Gregorianum* 89/2 (2008): 233–311. For Ratzinger's view of Vatican II during the council, see the 2009 reprint (orig. 1966) of Joseph Ratzinger, *Theological Highlights of Vatican II*, with an introduction by Thomas P. Rausch (New York/Mahwah, NJ: Paulist Press, 2009). For an example of Ratzinger's view of Vatican II in the mid-1970s, see Joseph Ratzinger, "Der Weltdienst der Kirche. Auswirkungen von 'Gaudium et spes' in letzten Jahrzehnt," *Communio* 4 (1975): 439–54; in English, "Church and World: An Inquiry into the Reception of Vatican Council II," in Joseph Ratzinger, *Principles of Catholic Theology: Building Stones for a Fundamental Theology*, trans. Mary Frances McCarthy (San Francisco: Ignatius, 1987), 378–93.

19. Joseph Ratzinger, *Das Neue Volk Gottes* (Düsseldorf: Patmos, 1969), 115.

20. See Ratzinger's commentary on the pastoral constitution *Gaudium et spes* in *Lexikon für Theologie und Kirche. Das Zweite Vatikanische Konzil*, vol. 3 (Freiburg: Herder, 1968): 313–54.

21. See Joseph Ratzinger, *Introduction to Christianity*, trans. J. R. Foster (New York: Herder and Herder, 1970).

22. Joseph Ratzinger, *Principles of Catholic Theology: Building Stones for a Fundamental Theology* (San Francisco: Ignatius, 1987), 372. The first publication of this article, "Der Weltdienst der Kirche. Auswirkungen von 'Gaudium et spes' in letzten Jahrzehnt," dates back to issue number 4 of the journal *Communio* (1975).

23. Ibid., 378.

24. Ibid., 381.

25. Ibid., 376.

26. See Joseph Ratzinger, "Zehn Jahre nach Konzilsbeginn— wo stehen wir?" *Dogma und Verkündigung* (Munich-Freiburg: Wewel, 1973), 439–47, quotation at 443.

27. Rush, *Still Interpreting Vatican II*, 16.

28. Gerald McCool, *The Neo-Thomists* (Milwaukee: Marquette University Press, 1994), 155–59, quotation at 159.

29. Gerald McCool, *From Unity to Pluralism: The Internal Evolution of Thomism* (New York: Fordham University Press, 1989), 225.

30. Marie-Dominique Chenu, *Une école de théologie: le Saulchoir* (Kain-lez-Tournai: Etiolles, 1937); *La théologie comme science au XIIIe siècle* (Paris: Vrin, 1957). See also Christophe Potworowski, *Contemplation and Incarnation: The Theology of Marie-Dominique Chenu* (Montreal: McGill-Queen's University Press, 2001).

31. Marie-Dominique Chenu, *Diario del Vaticano II: Note quotidiane al Concilio 1962–1963*, ed. Alberto Melloni (Bologna: Il Mulino, 1995), 75–76; original French, *Notes quotidiennes au Concile: Journal de Vatican II, 1962–1963* (Paris: Cerf, 1995).

32. Michael Quisinsky, *Geschichtlicher Glaube in einer geschichtlichen Welt. Der Beitrag von Marie-Dominique Chenu, Yves Congar und Henri-Marie Féret zum II. Vaticanum* (Münster: LIT, 2007).

33. Marie-Dominique Chenu, "Les signes des temps. Réflexion théologique," in *L'Église dans le monde de ce temps*, vol. 2, ed. Yves Congar and Michel Peuchmaurd (Paris: Cerf, 1967), 205.

34. Komonchak, "Augustine, Aquinas, or the Gospel *sine glossa*?" 108.

35. Marie-Dominique Chenu, "La fin de l'ère constantinienne," in *Un concile pour notre temps*, ed. Jean-Pierre Dubois-Dumee et al. (Paris: Cerf, 1961), 59–87. See also Marie-Dominique Chenu, *La chiesa nella storia. Fondamento e norma della interpretazione del concilio*, I–DOC 66–19 (October 12, 1966): 1–6.

36. Edward Schillebeeckx, *The Real Achievement of Vatican II*, trans. H. J. J. Vaughan (New York: Herder and Herder, 1966), 24.

37. Ibid., 37.

38. In his obituary of Congar in 1995, Avery Dulles said, "Vatican II could almost be called Congar's council." Dulles, quoted in Fergus Kerr, *Twentieth-Century Catholic Theologians: From Neoscholasticism to Nuptial Mysticism* (Malden, MA: Blackwell, 2007), 34. For Congar's importance, see *Yves Congar, Theologian of the Church*, ed. Gabriel Flynn (Louvain and Dudley, MA: Peeters; Grand Rapids: Eerdmans, 2005).

39. Yves Congar, *Chrétiens désunis. Principes d'un "oecumenisme" catholique* (Paris: Cerf, 1937); *Divided Christendom: A Catholic Study of the Problem of Reunion* (London: Bles, 1939); *Vraie et fausse réforme dans l'Église* (Paris: Cerf, 1950).

40. Yves Congar, *Journal d'un théologien 1946–1956*, ed. Étienne Fouilloux (Paris: Cerf, 2001).

41. Yves Congar, *Mon journal du concile*, ed. Éric Mahieu (Paris: Cerf, 2002), entry for December 9, 1962.

42. Ibid., entry for December 8, 1962.

43. Ibid., entry for October 5, 1965.

44. Yves Congar, "Vision de l'Église chez S. Thomas d'Aquin," *Revue de sciences philosophiques et théologiques* 62 (1978): 523–41; reprinted in Yves Congar, *Thomas d'Aquin: sa vision de théologie et de l'Église* (London: Variorum, 1984).

45. Yves Congar, "Regard sur le Concile Vatican II," in Yves Congar, *Le Concile Vatican II. Peuple de Dieu et corps du Christ* (Paris: Beauchesne, 1984), 49–72, quotation at 69.

46. Yves Congar, "Église et monde dans la perspective de Vatican II," in *L'Église dans le monde de ce temps*, vol. 3, ed. Yves Congar and Michel Peuchmaurd (Paris: Cerf, 1967), 31.

47. Karl Rahner, "Philosophy and Theology," in *Theological Investigations: Concerning Vatican II*, vol. 6 (London: Darton, Longman & Todd, 1974), 79–80.

48. Ibid., 80.

49. Bernard Lonergan, *Insight: A Study of Human Understanding* (New York: Philosophical Library, 1957); *Method in Theology* (New York: Herder and Herder, 1972).

50. Bernard Lonergan, "The Future of Thomism," in Bernard Lonergan, *A Second Collection*, ed. William F. J. Ryan and Bernard J. Tyrrell (London: Darton, Longman and Todd, 1974), 44 and 49.

51. Ibid., 161.

52. Ibid., 163.

53. Giuseppe Alberigo, "New Balances in the Church since the Synod," in *Synod 1985: An Evaluation*, ed. Giuseppe Alberigo and James Provost (Edinburgh: T. & T. Clark, 1986), 138–46, quotation at 138.

54. Alberto Melloni, "After the Council and the Episcopal Conferences: The Responses," in *Synod 1985: An Evaluation*, 14–23, quotations at 15 and 16.

55. Ibid., 22.

56. Joseph A. Komonchak, "The Theological Debate," in *Synod 1985: An Evaluation*, 53–63, quotation at 55.

57. Avery Dulles, "The Reception of Vatican II at the Extraordinary Synod of 1985," in *The Reception of Vatican II*, 349–63, quotation at 350. Also see *The Final Report of the 1985 Extraordinary Synod* (Washington, DC: National Conference of Catholic Bishops, 1986); Jean-Marie Tillard, "Final Report of the Last Synod," in *Synod 1985: An Evaluation*, 64–77.

58. *The Final Report of the 1985 Extraordinary Synod*, I.2 (emphasis mine).

59. Ibid., II.D.1.

60. See Eugenio Corecco's excellent essay "Aspects of the Reception of Vatican II in the Code of Canon Law," in *The Reception of Vatican II*, 249–96, esp. 295: "The fact that twenty years after the council the Code did not avoid this ambiguity is clearly not a reason for any sense of satisfaction." See also Bernard P. Prusak, *The Church*

Unfinished: Ecclesiology Through the Centuries (New York/Mahwah, NJ: Paulist Press, 2004).

61. On the debate on the episcopal conferences and the role of Cardinal Ratzinger, see Joseph A. Komonchak, "The Roman Working Paper on Episcopal Conferences," in *Episcopal Conferences. Historical, Canonical and Theological Studies*, ed. Thomas J. Reese (Washington, DC: Georgetown University Press, 1989), 177–204; Massimo Faggioli, "Prassi e norme relative alle conferenze episcopali tra concilio Vaticano II e post-concilio (1959–1998)," in *Synod and Synodality: Theology, History, Canon Law and Ecumenism in New Contact*, ed. Alberto Melloni and Silvia Scatena (Münster: LIT, 2005), 265–96.

62. Gilles Routhier, "L'Assemblée extraordinaire de 1985 du synode des évêques: moment charnière de relecture de Vatican II dans l'Église catholique," in *Le concile et la théologie. Perspectives pour le XXIe siècle*, ed. Philippe Bordeyne and Laurent Villemin (Paris: Cerf, 2006), 61–88, quotation at 80.

63. See Joseph A. Komonchak, "Interpreting the Council: Catholic Attitudes Toward Vatican II," in *Being Right: Conservative Catholics in America*, ed. Mary Jo Weaver and R. Scott Appleby (Bloomington: Indiana University Press, 1995), 17–36, quotation at 34. See also Joseph A. Komonchak, "Thomism and the Second Vatican Council," in *Continuity and Plurality in Catholic Theology: Essays in Honor of Gerald A. McCool*, ed. Anthony J. Cernera (Fairfield, CT: Sacred Heart University Press, 1998), 53–73.

64. David Tracy, *The Analogical Imagination: Christian Theology and the Culture of Pluralism* (New York: Crossroad, 1981), esp. 202–18 and 317–24. Also see Tracy's *Blessed Rage for Order* (New York: Seabury Press, 1975).

65. Gerald McCool, *From Unity to Pluralism: The Internal Evolution of Thomism* (New York: Fordham University Press, 1989), 216.

66. Walter Kasper, *Theology and Church* (New York: Crossroad, 1989), 1.

CHAPTER 5

1. Richard John Neuhaus, *The Catholic Moment: The Paradox of the Church in the Postmodern World* (San Francisco: Harper & Row, 1987), 39.

2. Ibid., 49.

3. Ibid., 61.

4. Hermann J. Pottmeyer, "A New Phase in the Reception of Vatican II: Twenty Years of Interpretation of the Council," in *The Reception of Vatican II*, ed. Giuseppe Alberigo, Jean-Pierre Jossua, and Joseph A. Komonchak (Washington, DC: Catholic University of America Press, 1987), 37.

5. Ibid., 41.

6. Note that coeditor Giuseppe Alberigo subsequently became the major editor for the five-volume *History of Vatican II*.

7. See Joseph Famerée, "Vers une histoire du Concile Vatican II," *Revue d'Histoire Ecclésiastique* 89 (1994): 638–41; Massimo Faggioli, "L'Institut pour les sciences religieuses de Bologne et la recherche sur Vatican II. Éléments pour une histoire de l'Histoire du Concile Vatican II dirigée par Giuseppe Alberigo," in *Christianisme, mission et cultures. L'arc en ciel des défis et des réponses XVIe–XXIe siècles*, ed. Paul Coulon and Alberto Melloni (Paris: Karthala, 2008), 61–74.

8. Giuseppe Alberigo, Preface, in *History of Vatican II*, vol. 1, *Announcing and Preparing Vatican Council II Toward a New Era in Catholicism*, ed. Joseph A. Komonchak (Maryknoll, NY: Orbis, 1996), xiii. See also *Per la storicizzazione del Vaticano II*, ed. Giuseppe Alberigo and Alberto Melloni, *Cristianesimo nella Storia* 13/3 (1992).

9. "À la veille du Concile Vatican II. Vota et réactions en Europe et dans le Catholicisme oriental" (Louvain et Louvain-la-Neuve, October 23–25, 1989); "Christianity and Churches on the Eve of Vatican II" (Houston, January 12–15, 1991); "Vatican II commence... Approches Francophones" (Lyon, March 27–29, 1992); "Der Beitrag der deutschsprächigen und osteuropäischen Länder zum Zweiten Vatikanischen Konzil" (Würzburg, December 17–19, 1993); "Les Commissions conciliaires à Vatican II" (Louvain et Louvain-la-Neuve, July 7–10, 1994); "Vatican II à Moscou (1959–1965)" (Moscow, March

30–April 2, 1995); "L'evento, l'esperienza e i documenti finali" (Bologna, December 12–15, 1996); "Vatican II au but? Espoirs, craintes, déceptions, perspectives" (Klingenthal/Strasbourg, March 11–14, 1999). See *L'officina bolognese 1953–2003*, ed. Giuseppe Alberigo (Bologna: EDB, 2004), 63–72.

10. *Sources locales de Vatican II*, ed. Jan Grootaers and Claude Soetens (Louvain: Peeters, 1990); *Cristianismo e iglesias de América Latina en vísperas del Vaticano II*, ed. José Oscar Beozzo (San José, Costa Rica: DEI, 1992); *À la veille du Concile Vatican II. Vota et réactions en Europe et dans le Catholicisme oriental*, ed. Mathijs Lamberigts and Claude Soetens (Louvain: Peeters, 1992); *Vatican II commence...Approches Francophones*, ed. Etienne Fouilloux (Louvain: Peeters, 1993); *Verso il concilio Vaticano II (1960–1962). Passaggi e problemi della preparazione conciliare*, ed. Giuseppe Alberigo and Alberto Melloni (Bologna: Il Mulino, 1993); *Il Vaticano II fra attese e celebrazione*, ed. Giuseppe Alberigo (Bologna: Il Mulino, 1995); *Der Beitrag der deutschsprächigen und osteuropäischen Länder zum zweiten vatikanischen Konzil*, ed. Klaus Wittstadt and Wim Verschooten (Louvain: Peeters, 1996); *Les commissions conciliaires à Vatican II*, ed. Mathijs Lamberigts, Claude Soetens, Jan Grootaers (Louvain: Peeters, 1996); *Zeugnis und Dialog. Die katholische Kirche in der neuzeitlichen Welt und das II. Vatikanische Konzil. Klaus Wittstadt zum 60. Geburtstag*, ed. Wolfgang Weiß (Würzburg: Echter, 1996); *Vatican II in Moscow (1959–1962)*, ed. Alberto Melloni (Leuven: Bibliotheek van de Faculteit Godgeleerdheid, 1997); *L'evento e le decisioni. Studi sulle dinamiche del concilio Vaticano II*, ed. Maria Teresa Fattori and Alberto Melloni (Bologna: Il Mulino, 1997); *Experience, Organisations and Bodies at Vatican II*, ed. Maria Teresa Fattori and Alberto Melloni (Leuven: Bibliotheek van de Faculteit Godgeleerdheid, 1999); *Volti di fine concilio. Studi di storia e teologia sulla conclusione del Vaticano II*, ed. Joseph Dorè and Alberto Melloni (Bologna: Il Mulino, 2000).

11. *History of Vatican II*, 5 vols., ed. Giuseppe Alberigo; English version, ed. Joseph A. Komonchak (Louvain: Peeters, 1995–2006; Maryknoll, NY: Orbis, 1995–2006). The work was published in Italian, English, French, German, Spanish, Portuguese, and Russian.

12. On the genesis of the *Acta et documenta Concilio Oecumenico Vaticano II apparando. Series I–Series II*, and of the *Acta Synodalia Sac-*

rosancti Concilii Oecumenici Vaticani II, 33 vols. (Vatican City: Typis Polyglottis Vaticanis, 1970–1999), see Massimo Faggioli and Giovanni Turbanti, "Introduzione," in *Il concilio inedito. Fonti del Vaticano II*, ed. Massimo Faggioli and Giovanni Turbanti (Bologna: Il Mulino, 2001), 7–34.

13. See Gilles Routhier, *La réception d'un concile* (Paris: Cerf, 1993).

14. For bibliographies on Vatican II see Massimo Faggioli, "Concilio Vaticano II: Bollettino bibliografico (2000–2002)," *Cristianesimo nella Storia* 24 (2003): 335–60; "Concilio Vaticano II: Bollettino bibliografico (2002–2005)," *Cristianesimo nella Storia* 26 (2005): 743–67; "Council Vatican II: Bibliographical Overview 2005–2007," *Cristianesimo nella Storia* 29 (2008): 567–610; "Council Vatican II: Bibliographical Overview 2007–2010," *Cristianesimo nella Storia* 32 (2011): 755–91.

15. *Herders Theologischer Kommentar zum Zweiten Vatikanischen Konzil*, ed. Hans Jochen Hilberath and Peter Hünermann, 5 vols. (Freiburg i.B: Herder, 2004–5). Still very useful and authoritative for the commentary on the documents of Vatican II are the last three volumes of the second edition of the *Lexikon für Theologie und Kirche*, ed. Josef Höfer and Karl Rahner (Freiburg i.B: Herder, 1966–68). An appendix to the new five-volume *Kommentar* is *Das Zweiten Vatikanische Konzil und die Zeichen der Zeit heute*, ed. Peter Hünermann (Freiburg i.B: Herder, 2006).

16. See http://asv.vatican.va/en/fond/1_fond.htm.

17. Said by Cardinal Camillo Ruini (then vicar for the Diocese of Rome and president of the Italian Bishops' Conference), in Rome, June 17, 2005, while introducing to the media Agostino Marchetto's *Il concilio ecumenico Vaticano II. Contrappunto per la sua storia* (Vatican City: Libreria Editrice Vaticana, 2005). This collection of book reviews has been translated into English and Russian between 2008 and 2010. The English edition is *The Second Vatican Ecumenical Council: A Counterpoint for the History of the Council*, trans. Kenneth D. Whitehead (Scranton, PA: University of Scranton Press, 2010). From Cardinal Ruini, also see his introduction to Karol Wojtyla, *Alle fonti del rinnovamento. Studio sull'attuazione del Concilio Vaticano II*, foreword and introduction by Cardinal

Camillo Ruini, ed. Flavio Felice (Vatican City: Libreria Editrice Vaticana, 2001); Polish edition, *U Podstaw Odnowy Stadium o realizacji Vaticanum II* (Krakow: Polskie Towarzystwo Teologiczne, 1972, 1981). The Italian edition was later reprinted in 2007 by Fondazione Novae Terrae-Rubbettino, in Soveria Mannelli, Italy.

18. *Spiritual Testament of John Paul II*, at http://www.vatican.va/gpII/documents/testamento-jp-ii_20050407_en.html.

19. See the new edition of Joseph Ratzinger, *Theological Highlights of Vatican II* (New York/Mahwah, NJ: Paulist Press, 2009).

20. See Benedict XVI, Christmas Address to the Roman Curia, December 22, 2005, in *Insegnamenti di Benedetto XVI*, vol. 1 (2005) (Vatican City: Libreria Editrice Vaticana, 2006), 1018–32, and at http://www.vatican.va/holy_father/benedict_xvi/speeches/2005/december/documents/hf_ben_xvi_spe_20051222_roman-curia_en.html.

21. See Umberto Betti, "Cronistoria della Costituzione," in *La Chiesa del Vaticano II. Studi e commenti intorno alla Costituzione dommatica "Lumen Gentium"* (Florence: Vallecchi, 1965), 131–54; Gerard Philips, *L'Église et son mystère au IIe Concile du Vatican. Histoire, text et commentaire de la constitution "Lumen gentium"* (Paris: Desclée, 1966–68); Antonio Acerbi, *Due ecclesiologie. Ecclesiologia giuridica ed ecclesiologia di comunione nella Lumen gentium* (Bologna: EDB, 1975); *Constitutionis Dogmaticae "Lumen Gentium" synopsis historica*, ed. Giuseppe Alberigo and Franca Magistretti (Bologna: Istituto per le scienze religiose, 1975).

22. Among the most recent contributions see Daniele Gianotti, *I Padri della Chiesa al concilio Vaticano II. La teologia patristica nella Lumen gentium* (Bologna: EDB, 2010).

23. See Richard Gaillardetz, *The Church in the Making: Lumen Gentium, Christus Dominus, Orientalium Ecclesiarum* (New York/Mahwah NJ: Paulist Press, 2006), 26.

24. No. 4 of *Nota Explicativa Praevia*, which appears at the end of *Lumen Gentium*.

25. Hermann J. Pottmeyer, *Towards a Papacy in Communion: Perspectives from Vatican Councils I and II*, trans. Matthew J. O'Connell (New York: Crossroad, 1998), 110.

26. Klaus Schatz, *Papal Primacy: From Its Origins to the Present*, trans. John A. Otto and Linda M. Maloney (Collegeville, MN: Liturgical Press, 1996. Original German, Wurzburg: Echter, 1990), 170. On the ecclesiology of communion and its ancient roots, see also Jean-Marie Roger Tillard, *Church of Churches: The Ecclesiology of Communion*, trans. R. C. De Peaux (Collegeville, MN: Liturgical Press, 1992; original French, Paris: Cerf, 1987).

27. Hervé Marie Legrand, "Les évêques, les *églises locales* et l'église *entière*. Évolutions institutionnelles depuis Vatican II et chantiers actuels de recherche," *Revue de Sciences philosophiques et théologiques* 85 (2001): 461–509; Hervé Marie Legrand, "Lo sviluppo di chiese soggetto: un'istanza del Vaticano II. Fondamenti teologici e riflessioni," in *L'ecclesiologia del Vaticano II: dinamismi e prospettive*, ed. Giuseppe Alberigo (Bologna: EDB, 1981), 129–63. See also Gilles Routhier, "Beyond Collegiality: The Local Church Left Behind by the Second Vatican Council," Catholic Theological Society of America, *Proceedings* 62 (2007), 1–15.

28. See Ciro García Fernández, "De la 'teología de los laicos' de 'Lumen gentium' a los 'movimientos eclesiales' posconciliares," *Burgense* 48/1 (2007): 45–82; Gilles Routhier, "Une histoire qui témoigne du reflux du thème du laïcat?" in *Vatican II sous le regard des historiens*, ed. Christoph Theobald (Paris: Médiasèvres, 2006), 95–125.

29. Gaillardetz, *The Church in the Making*, 22.

30. See Alexandra von Teuffenbach, *Die Bedeutung des subsistit in (LG 8). Zum Selbstverständnis der katholischen Kirche* (Munich: Herbert Utz, 2002).

31. See Giuseppe Ruggieri, "Beyond an Ecclesiology of Polemics," in *History of Vatican II*, vol. 3, *The Mature Council: Second Period and Intercession, September 1963–September 1964*, ed. Joseph A. Komonchak (Maryknoll, NY: Orbis, 2000), 281–357.

32. See Mauro Velati, "L'ecumenismo al concilio: Paolo VI e l'approvazione di Unitatis redintegratio," *Cristianesimo nella Storia* 26/2 (2005): 427–76; see also the appendix with the diary entries of Johannes Willebrands in the decisive moments of the debate on *Unitatis redintegratio*.

33. Luigi Sartori, "Osservazioni sull'ermeneutica del 'subsistit in' proposta da Alexandra von Teuffenbach," *Rassegna di Teologia* XLV/2 (marzo–aprile 2004): 279–81; Emmanuel Lanne, "Le quarantième anniversaire de la promulgation du Décret sur l'oecumenisme Unitatis redintegratio," *Irénikon* 2004/4:548–66; Karim Schelkens, "Lumen gentium's 'subsistit in' revisited: The Catholic Church and Christian Unity After Vatican II," *Theological Studies* 69 (2008): 875–93.

34. Congregation for the Doctrine of the Faith, "Responses to Some Questions Regarding Certain Aspects of the Doctrine of the Church," June 29, 2007, at http://www.vatican.va/roman_curia/congregations/cfaith/documents/rc_con_cfaith_doc_20070629_responsa-quaestiones_en.html.

35. See Francis A. Sullivan, "The Meaning of *Subsistit in* as Explained by the Congregation for the Doctrine of Faith," *Theological Studies* 69/1 (2008): 116–24; Wolfgang Thönissen, "Über Einheit und Wahrheit der Kirche. Zum Verständnis des "subsitit in" gegenwärtigen ökumenischen Disput," *Catholica* 3/2007: 230–40.

36. About the recent developments in ecumenism, its gains, and the remaining issues, see Walter Kasper, *Harvesting the Fruits: Aspects of Christian Faith in Ecumenical Dialogue* (London: Continuum, 2009).

37. See Mathijs Lamberigts, "The Liturgy Debate," in *History of Vatican II*, vol. 2, *The Formation of the Council's Identity, First Period and Intercession, October 1962–September 1963*, ed. Joseph A. Komonchak (Maryknoll, NY: Orbis, 1998), 107–66; Reiner Kaczinsky, "Toward the Reform of the Liturgy," in *History of Vatican II*, vol. 3, *The Mature Council, Second Period and Intercession, September 1963–September 1964* (Maryknoll, NY: Orbis 2000), 192–256.

38. See, for example, Maria Paiano, *Liturgia e società nel Novecento: Percorsi del movimento liturgico di fronte ai processi di secolarizzazione* (Rome: Storia e Letteratura, 2000).

39. See, for example, the following articles in *Liturgisches Jahrbuch* 53 (2003): Joseph Ratzinger, "40 Jahre Konstitution über die Heilige Liturgie. Rückblick und Vorblick," 209–21; Jürgen Bärsch, "'Von Grösstem Gewicht für die Liturgiefeier ist die Heilige Schrift' (SC 24): Zur Bedeutung der Bibel im Kontext des Gottesdienstes," 222–41;

Andreas Odenthal, "Häresie der Formlosigkeit durch ein 'Konzil der Buchhalter': Überlegungen zur Kritik an der Liturgiereform nach 40 Jahren 'Sacrosanctum Concilium,'" 242–57.

40. Hans Jochen Hilberath and Peter Hünermann, eds., *Herders Theologischer Kommentar zum Zweiten Vatikanischen Konzil*, 5 vols. (Freiburg: Herder, 2004–5).

41. Reiner Kaczynski, "Toward the Reform of the Liturgy," in *History of Vatican II*, vol. 3, *The Mature Council*, esp. 220–34.

42. See Reiner Kaczynski, "Theologischer Kommentar zur Konstitution über die Heilige Liturgie Sacrosanctum Concilium," in *Herders Theologischer Kommentar*, 2:9–227, esp. 63 where he quotes Angelus A. Häussling, originally published in "Pascha-Mysterium: Kritisches zu einem Beitrag in der dritten Auflage des Lexikon für Theologie und Kirche," *Archiv für Liturgiewissenschaft* 41 (1999): 157–65.

43. See Piero Marini, *A Challenging Reform: Realizing the Vision of the Liturgical Renewal, 1963–1975*, ed. Mark R. Francis, John R. Page, and Keith F. Pecklers (Collegeville, MN: Liturgical Press, 2007); John Baldovin, *Reforming the Liturgy: A Response to the Critics* (Collegeville, MN: Liturgical Press, 2008).

44. See Aidan Nichols, *Looking at the Liturgy: A Critical View of Its Contemporary Form* (San Francisco: Ignatius, 1996); Martin Mosebach, *Häresie der Formlosigkeit: Die römische Liturgie und ihr Feind*, expanded ed. (Munich: Hanser, 2007); Italian trans., *Eresia dell'informe: La liturgia romana e il suo nemico* (Siena: Cantagalli, 2009); Pamela Jackson, *An Abundance of Graces: Reflections on Sacrosanctum Concilium* (Mundelein, IL: Hillenbrand, 2004); Pamela Jackson, "Theology of the Liturgy," in *Vatican II: Renewal within Tradition*, ed. Matthew L. Lamb and Matthew Levering (New York-Oxford: Oxford University Press, 2008), 101–28.

45. John W. O'Malley, *What Happened at Vatican II* (Cambridge, MA: Belknap Press, 2008), 300–301.

46. See Patrick Prétot, "La Constitution sur la liturgie: Une herméneutique de la tradition liturgique," in *Vatican II et la théologie: Perspectives pour le XXIe siècle*, ed. Philippe Bordeyne and Laurent Villemin (Paris, Cerf: 2006), 17–34, quotation at 20.

47. See John Baldovin, *Reforming the Liturgy*; Rita Ferrone, *Liturgy: Sacrosanctum Concilium* (New York/Mahwah, NJ: Paulist

Press, 2007), esp. 19–50; Alberto Melloni, "Sacrosanctum Concilium 1963–2003: Lo spessore storico della riforma liturgica e la ricezione del Vaticano II," *Rivista liturgica* 90 (2002): 915–30; Andrea Grillo, *La nascita della liturgia nel XX secolo. Saggio sul rapporto tra movimento liturgico e (post-) modernità* (Assisi: Cittadella, 2003).

48. See Massimo Faggioli, "Concilio Vaticano II: Bollettino bibliografico (2002–2005)," *Cristianesimo nella Storia* 26 (2005): 743–67; and "Council Vatican II: Bibliographical Overview 2005–2007," *Cristianesimo nella Storia* 29 (2008): 567–610.

49. Joseph Ratzinger (Benedikt XVI), "Zum Eröffnungsband meiner Schriften," in *Gesammelte Schriften*, vol. 11, *Theologie der Liturgie* (Freiburg: Herder, 2008, second edition).

50. Rita Ferrone, "Virgil & the Vigil," *Commonweal* (April 10, 2009): 12–13. Related to this debate on the interpretation of the liturgical reform of Vatican II is an initiative that takes its name from a December 14, 2009, article in *America* by Michael G. Ryan: "What If We Just Said Wait? The Case for a Grass-roots Review of the New Roman Missal." The initiative has an online petition urging delay of the new translation to allow further review. See http://www.whatif wejustsaidwait.org.

51. For a synthetic description of the entrenched and conflicting narratives about Vatican II, see Peter Steinfels, *A People Adrift: The Crisis of the Roman Catholic Church in America* (New York: Simon and Schuster, 2003), 34–36.

52. See Agostino Marchetto's book review of the second volume of the *History of Vatican II*, in *Osservatore Romano*, November 13, 1997, and in *Apollinaris* LXX (1997), 331–51; now republished in his *Il Concilio Ecumenico Vaticano II*, 102–19. All the other historians and theologians had reviewed favorably the *History of Vatican II*: in the same "Roman milieu," see, for example, Giacomo Martina, in *La Civiltà Cattolica* CXLVII/2 (1996): 153–60 and in *Archivum Historiae Pontificiae* XXXV (1997): 356–59.

53. For the use of the idea of "event" for the historiography of Vatican II, see Étienne Fouilloux, "Histoire et événement: Vatican II," in *Per la storicizzazione del Vaticano II*, 515–38. Also see Peter Hünermann, "Il concilio Vaticano II come evento," and Joseph A.

Komonchak, "Riflessioni storiografiche sul Vaticano II come evento," in *L'evento e le decisioni. Studi sulle dinamiche del concilio Vaticano II*, ed. Maria Teresa Fattori and Alberto Melloni (Bologna: Il Mulino, 1997), 63–92 and 417–40.

54. Philippe Chenaux, "Recensione storiografica circa le prospettive di lettura del Vaticano II," *Lateranum* LXXII/1 (2006): 161–75, quotation at 168. A similar perspective in Giovanni Maria Vian (since September 2007 editor-in-chief of *Osservatore Romano*), "La dinamica tra evento e decisioni nella storiografia conciliare," *Annuarium Historiae Conciliorum* 37/2 (2005): 357–74.

55. See, for example, David Berger, "Wider die Veteranensentimentalität. Zur Rezeption des Zweiten Vatikanischen Konzils," *Die Neue Ordnung* 58 (2004): 108–20; and David Berger, "'Das Geschick der Kirche steht dabei auf dem Spiel....' Zur Interpretation des Zweiten Vatikanischen Konzils," *Theologisches* 35/12 (Dezember 2005): 765–81.

56. See *Penser Vatican II quarante ans après*. Actes du VIe congrès théologique de "Sì Sì No No" (Versailles: Courrier de Rome, 2004); Dominic Bourmaud, *Cent ans de modernisme. Généalogie du concile Vatican II* (Étampes: Clovis, 2003).

57. Typical of this sentiment is Hans Küng's memoir, *My Struggle for Freedom* (Grand Rapids, MI: Eerdmans, 2003).

58. Avery Dulles, "Vatican II: The Myth and the Reality," *America*, February 24, 2003, 7–11.

59. John O'Malley, "The Style of Vatican II," *America*, February 24, 2003, 12–15. The debate between Dulles and O'Malley is also in two other articles, both in *America*, March 31, 2003: Avery Dulles, "Vatican II: Substantive Teaching," 14–17, and John O'Malley, "Vatican II: Official Norms," 11–14.

60. Benedict XVI, Christmas Address, December 22, 2005.

61. Joseph Ratzinger, with Vittorio Messori, *The Ratzinger Report: An Exclusive Interview on the State of the Church*, trans. Salvator Attanasio and Graham Harrison (San Francisco: Ignatius, 1985), 35.

62. Benedict XVI, Christmas Address, December 22, 2005.

63. Ibid. On the hermeneutical criteria for the *History of Vatican II*, see Giuseppe Alberigo, "Critères herméneutiques pour une histoire de Vatican II," in *À la Veille du Concile Vatican II. Vota et*

Notes

Réactions en Europe et dans le Catholicisme oriental (Louvain: Peeters, 1992), 12–23; now in Giuseppe Alberigo, *Transizione epocale. Studi sul Concilio Vaticano II* (Bologna: Il Mulino, 2009), 29–45.

64. For the constitutional characteristics of Vatican II, see Peter Hünermann, "Der Text: Werden—Gestalt—Bedeutung. Eine Hermeneutische Reflexion," in *Herders Theologischer Kommentar zum Zweiten Vatikanischen Konzil*, ed. Hans Jochen Hilberath and Peter Hünermann, 5 vols. (Freiburg: Herder, 2004–5), 5:5–101, esp. 11–17 and 85–87.

65. Joseph A. Komonchak, "Novelty in Continuity. Pope Benedict's Interpretation of Vatican II," *America*, February 2, 2009, 10–16. See also Joseph Komonchak, "Benedict XVI and the Interpretation of Vatican II," *Cristianesimo nella Storia* 28/2 (2007): 323–37; Lieven Boeve, "'La vraie réception de Vatican II n'a pas encore commencé.' J. Ratzinger, Révélation et autorité de Vatican II," *Ephemerides Theologicae Lovanienses* 85/4 (2009): 305–39.

66. See *Herausforderung Aggiornamento: zur Rezeption Vatican-ischen Konzils*, ed. Antonio Autiero (Altenberge: Oros, 2000); *Unfinished Journey: The Church 40 Years after Vatican II, Essays for John Wilkins*, ed. Austin Ivereigh (New York: Continuum, 2003); *Zweites Vaticanum—vergessene Anstöße, gegenwärtige Fortschreibungen*, ed. Gunther Wassilowsky (Freiburg: Herder, 2004); *Zweites Vatikanisches Konzil—Ende oder Anfang?* ed. Alfred E. Hierold (Münster: LIT, 2004); *Vatican II: A Forgotten Future?* in *Concilium* 4/2005, ed. Alberto Melloni and Christoph Theobald; *Vatican II: Did Anything Happen?* ed. David G. Schultenover (New York: Continuum, 2007).

67. Ormond Rush, *Still Interpreting Vatican II: Some Hermeneutical Principles* (New York/Mahwah, NJ: Paulist Press, 2004), x–xi.

68. Gilles Routhier, *Vatican II. Herméneutique et reception* (Montreal: Fides, 2006), 211; see also Routhier, *La reception d'un concile* (Paris: Cerf, 1993).

69. Routhier, *Vatican II*, 421.

70. Ladislas Orsy, *Receiving the Council: Theological and Canonical Insights and Debates* (Collegeville, MN: Liturgical Press, 2009), 4.

71. Ibid., 5.

72. Peter Hünermann, "Der Text: Werden—Gestalt—Bedeutung," in *Theologischer Kommentar*, 5:5–101, esp. 11–17 and 85–87, quotation at 12.

73. Ibid., 15–16.

74. Ibid., 17.

75. Christoph Theobald, *La réception du concile Vatican II* [vol. 1]. *Accéder à la source* (Paris: Cerf, 2009); [vol. 2] *L'Église dans l'histoire et la société* (Paris: Cerf, forthcoming). See also Theobald, *"Dans les traces…"* *de la constitution "Dei Verbum" du concile Vatican II. Bible, théologie et pratiques de lecture* (Paris: Cerf, 2009).

76. Theobald, *La réception du concile Vatican II*, vol. 1, 891.

77. Ibid., 893 and 896. On the hermeneutical balance between the four constitutions of Vatican II in the interpretation of the council, see *Le concile et la théologie. Perspectives pour le XXIe siècle*, ed. Philippe Bordeyne and Laurent Villemin (Paris: Cerf, 2006).

78. See Giuseppe Alberigo, "Criteri ermeneutici per una storia del Vaticano II" e "Fedeltà e creatività nella ricezione del Concilio Vaticano II. Criteri ermeneutici," in Giuseppe Alberigo, *Transizione epocale*, 29–45 and 47–69.

79. For a historiographical-ecclesiological appreciation of the five-volume *History of Vatican II* edited by Alberigo, see *Vatican II sous le regard des historiens*, ed. Christoph Theobald (Paris: Médiasèvres, 2006).

80. An example of this revisionistic attempt is *Vatican II: Renewal within Tradition*, ed. Matthew L. Lamb and Matthew Levering (New York: Oxford University Press, 2008).

81. O'Malley, *What Happened at Vatican II*, 311. Also see O'Malley, "Vatican II: Did Anything Happen?" *Theological Studies* 67 (2006): 3–33.

CHAPTER 6

1. Gerald W. Schlabach, *Unlearning Protestantism: Sustaining Christian Community in an Unstable Age* (Grand Rapids, MI: Brazos Press, 2010), 120.

2. An example of this "originalist" view is Kenneth D. Whitehead, "Vatican II Then and Now: A Review Essay on John O'Malley, SJ's *What Happened at Vatican II*," *Nova et Vetera* 8/2 (2010): 467–83.

3. John W. O'Malley, *What Happened at Vatican II* (Cambridge, MA: Belknap Press, 2008), 312.

4. The lecture of 1965 recalled an earlier essay about the reception of an ecumenical council by Karl Rahner, "Chalkedon, Ende oder Anfang?" in *Das Konzil von Chalkedon. Geschichte und Gegenwart*, ed. Alois Grillmeier and Heinrich Bacht (Wurzburg: Echter-Verlag, 1954). See also Karl Rahner, *Das Konzil—ein neuer Beginn. Vortrag beim Festakt zum Abschluss des II. Vatikanischen Konzils im Herkulessaal der Residenz in München am 12. Dez. 1965* (Freiburg: Herder, 1966).

5. Karl Rahner, "The Abiding Significance of the Second Vatican Council," in Karl Rahner, *Concern for the Church* (Theological Investigations XX), trans. Edward Quinn (New York: Crossroad, 1981), 90–102, quotation at 90–91.

6. Ibid., 96. See also Karl Rahner, "Towards a Fundamental Theological Interpretation of Vatican II," *Theological Studies* 40/4 (December 1979): 716–27; reprinted with the title "Basic Theological Interpretation of the Second Vatican Council," in Rahner, *Concern for the Church*, 77–89.

7. Raimon Panikkar embraced this interpretation in his vision of the evolution of Christendom to Christianity to "Christianness." He wrote: "This is what has prompted me to call not for a Vatican III but for a Second Council of Jerusalem." Raimon Panikkar, "The Jordan, the Tiber, and the Ganges: Three Kairological Moments of Christic Self-Consciousness," in *The Myth of Christian Uniqueness: Toward a Pluralistic Theology of Religions*, ed. John Hick and Paul F. Knitter (Maryknoll, NY: Orbis, 1987), 89–116, quotation at 89.

8. Christoph Theobald, *La réception du concile Vatican II, I. Accéder à la source* (Paris: Cerf, 2009), 670.

9. Karl Lehmann, "Das II. Vatikanum—Ein Wegweiser. Verständnis—Rezeption—Bedeutung," in *Das Zweite Vatikanische Konzil und die Zeichen der Zeit heute*, ed. Peter Hünermann (Freiburg i.B: Herder, 2006), 11–26, quotation at 12.

10. Ibid., 18.

11. Ormond Rush, *Still Interpreting Vatican II: Some Hermeneutical Principles* (New York/Mahwah, NJ: Paulist Press, 2004), 71.

12. See Gilles Routhier, *La reception d'un concile* (Paris: Cerf, 1993).

13. Ladislas Orsy, *Receiving the Council: Theological and Canonical Insights and Debates* (Collegeville, MN: Liturgical Press, 2009), 4.

14. See Walter Kasper, "'Wieder die Unglückspropheten': Die Vision des Konzils für die Erneuerung der Kirche," *Communio* 19 (1990): 514–26; now in Walter Kasper, *Die Kirche Jesu Christi. Schriften zur Ekklesiologie, I* (Walter Kasper Gesammelte Schriften, 11) (Freiburg: Herder, 2008), 238–53.

15. See Alberto Melloni, "Breve guida ai giudizi sul Vaticano II," in *Chi ha paura del Vaticano II?* ed. Alberto Melloni and Giuseppe Ruggieri (Rome: Carocci, 2009), 107–45.

16. Gilles Routhier, *Vatican II. Herméneutique et Réception* (Montreal: Fides, 2006), 421. About this, see also Hervé-Marie Legrand, "Les évêques, les Églises locales et l'Église entière. Évolutions institutionelles depuis Vatican II et chantiers actuels de recherche," *Revue de Sciences philosophiques et théologiques* 85 (2001), 461–509.

17. Hermann J. Pottmeyer, *Towards a Papacy in Communion: Perspectives from Vatican Councils I & II* (New York: Crossroad, 1998), 110.

18. See Rush, *Still Interpreting Vatican II*, 69–85.

19. About this, see *L'Autorité et les Autorités. L'hermenéutique théologique de Vatican II*, ed. Gilles Routhier and Guy Jobin (Paris: Cerf, 2010).

20. Herbert Vorgrimler, Introduction, *Commentary on the Documents of Vatican II*, trans. Lalit Adolphus, Kevin Smyth, and Richard Strachan (London: Burns & Oates; New York: Herder & Herder, 1967–69), vol. 1, viii; original German: *Lexikon Für Theologie und Kirche. Das Zweite Vatikanische Konzil: Konstitutionen, Dekrete, und Erklärungen. Lateinisch und Deutsch Kommentare*, 3 vols., Freiburg: Herder, 1966–68).

21. See Giuseppe Ruggieri, "Recezione e interpretazione del Vaticano II. Le ragioni di un dibattito," in *Chi ha paura del Vaticano II?*

ed. Alberto Melloni and Giuseppe Ruggieri (Rome: Carocci, 2009), 33–41.

22. *The Final Report of the 1985 Extraordinary Synod* (Washington, DC: National Conference of Catholic Bishops, 1986), 22.

23. See O'Malley, *What Happened at Vatican II*, 43–48.

24. Rush, *Still Interpreting Vatican II*, 35–51.

25. For the conception of the relations between conciliar texts and Vatican II as a whole, see Christoph Theobald, "Introduction," in *Vatican II. L'integralité. Editio bilingue révisée* (Paris, 2002), i–xxxiv; also *"Dans les traces…" de la constitution "Dei Verbum" du concile Vatican II. Bible, théologie et pratiques de lecture* (Paris: Cerf 2009).

26. Christoph Theobald, "Mise en perspective," in *Vatican II sous le regard des historiens*, Christoph Theobald, ed. (Paris: Médiasèvres, 2006), 3–23, quotation at 12–13. See also Theobald, "Enjeux herméneutiques des débats sur l'histoire du concile Vatican II," *Cristianesimo nella Storia* 28/2 (2007): 359–80.

27. Christoph Theobald, *La réception du concile Vatican II, I. Accéder à la source*, 769.

28. Jared Wicks, "Vatican II on Revelation—From Behind the Scenes," *Theological Studies* 71 (2010): 637–50, quotation at 639. For the central role of *Dei Verbum* according to Wicks, see also his book *Doing Theology* (New York/Mahwah, NJ: Paulist Press, 2009).

29. See Benedict XVI's postsynodal apostolic exhortation *Verbum Domini* (September 30, 2010), esp. par. 3, "From Dei Verbum to the Synod on the Word of God," at http://www.vatican.va/holy_father/benedict_xvi/apost_exhortations/documents/hf_ben-xvi_exh_20100930_verbum-domini_en.pdf.

30. Rush, *Still Interpreting Vatican II*, 42–43. For Rush's view of the relationship between revelation and theology in terms of *sensus ecclesiae* and *sensus fidelium*, see his volume *The Eyes of Faith: The Sense of the Faithful & the Church's Reception of Revelation* (Washington, DC: Catholic University of America Press, 2009).

31. See John W. O'Malley, *Four Cultures of the West* (Cambridge, MA: Belknap Press, 2004).

32. O'Malley, *What Happened at Vatican II*, 310.

33. Gilles Routhier, "Il Vaticano II come stile," *La Scuola Cattolica* 136 (2008): 5–32, quotation at 32.

34. Peter Hünermann, "Der Text: Werden—Gestalt—Bedeutung. Eine Hermeneutische Reflexion," in *Herders Theologischer Kommentar zum Zweiten Vatikanischen Konzil*, ed. Hans Jochen Hilberath and Peter Hünermann, 5 vols. (Freiburg: Herder, 2004–5), 5:5–101, esp. 11–17 and 85–87; quotation at 15, 16, and 17. See also a more nuanced version of this view in Peter Hünermann, "Der Text. Eine Ergänzung zur Hermeneutik des II. Vatikanischen Konzils," *Cristianesimo nella Storia* 28/2 (2007): 339–58.

35. Hünermann, "Der Text: Werden—Gestalt—Bedeutung," 85.

36. Ruggieri, "Recezione e interpretazione del Vaticano II," 41–42.

37. O'Malley, *What Happened at Vatican II*, 312.

38. See Michael Quisinsky, *Geschichtlicher Glaube in einer geschichtlichen Welt: Der Beitrag von M.-D. Chenu, Y. Congar und H.-M. Féret zum II. Vaticanum* (Münster: LIT, 2007).

39. Joseph A. Komonchak, "Interpreting the Council: Catholic Attitudes Toward Vatican II," in *Being Right: Conservative Catholics in America*, ed. Mary Jo Weaver and R. Scott Appleby (Bloomington: Indiana University Press, 1995), 17–36, quotation at 19.

40. See James Hitchcock, *Catholicism and Modernity: Confrontation or Capitulation?* (Ann Arbor, MI: Servant Books, 1979), 1–14.

41. See Hubert Jedin, *A History of the Council of Trent*, trans. Ernest Graf, 4 vols. (London: T. Nelson, 1957–61).

42. For example, there was a gap between the procedures established at Trent for the bishops' appointment and the actual procedures as they were interpreted by post-Trent popes and Roman Curia in the Tridentine era; see Massimo Faggioli, "La disciplina di nomina dei vescovi prima e dopo il concilio di Trento," *Società e Storia* 92 (2001): 221–56; and Massimo Faggioli, "Problemi relativi alle nomine episcopali dal concilio di Trento al pontificato di Urbano VIII," *Cristianesimo nella Storia* 21/3 (2000): 531–64. For a more general perspective, see John W. O'Malley, *Trent and All That: Renaming Catholicism in the Early Modern Era* (Cambridge, MA: Harvard University Press, 2002).

43. Joseph A. Komonchak, "The Council of Trent at the Second Vatican Council," in *From Trent to Vatican II: Historical and Theological Perspectives*, ed. Raymond F. Bulman and Frederick J. Parrella (New York: Oxford University Press, 2006), 61–80, quotation at 76.

44. See Massimo Faggioli, "Vatican Council II between Documents and Spirit: The Case of the New Catholic Movements," in *Proceedings of the Vatican II Symposium*, University of Southern California (Los Angeles, February 27–28, 2009), ed. by James Heft (forthcoming).

45. Joseph Ratzinger, "Weltoffene Kirche?" in Joseph Ratinzger, *Das neue Volk Gottes. Entwürfe zur Ekklesiologie* (Düsseldorf: Patmos-Verl., 1969), 300.

46. Joseph Ratzinger, with Vittorio Messori, *The Ratzinger Report: An Exclusive Interview on the State of the Church*, trans. Salvator Attanasio and Graham Harrison (San Francisco: Ignatius, 1985), 40.

47. See O'Malley, *What Happened at Vatican II*, 292.

48. See Peter Hünermann, "Il Concilio Vaticano II come evento," in *L'evento e le decisioni. Studi sulle dinamiche del concilio Vaticano II*, ed. Alberto Melloni and Maria Teresa Fattori (Bologna: Il Mulino, 1997), 63–92.

49. At Vatican II, the council fathers came from 116 countries: 33 percent from Western Europe, 23 percent from Latin America, 12 percent from North America, 9 percent from sub-Saharan Africa, 7 percent from Eastern Europe, 4 percent from the Arab world, and 12 percent from Asia and Australia combined. This international character of Vatican II was unprecedented, and not only in the number of non-Western participants.

50. See Klaus Schatz, *Allgemeine Konzilien—Brennpunkte der Kirchengeschichte* (Paderborn: Ferdinand Schöningh, 1999); Christopher M. Bellitto, *The General Councils: A History of the Twenty-One Church Councils from Nicaea to Vatican II* (New York/Mahwah, NJ: Paulist Press, 2002); Joseph F. Kelly, *The Ecumenical Councils of the Catholic Church: A History* (Collegeville, MN: Liturgical Press, 2009).

51. See Hans Küng, chart, "Paradigm Shifts in Christianity," in *Christianity: Essence, History, and Future* (New York: Continuum, 1995), no page; original German, *Das Christentum: Wesen und Geschichte*

(Munich: Piper, 1994). See also *Paradigm Change in Theology: A Symposium for the Future*, ed. Hans Küng and David Tracy (New York: Crossroad, 1989); original German *Theologie—wohin?* and *Das neue Paradigma von Theologie* (Zürich: Benziger, 1984).

52. See Lieven Boeve, "Une histoire de changement et conflit des paradigmes théologiques? Vatican II et sa réception entre continuité et discontinuité." A paper presented at the conference "La théologie catholique entre intransigeance et renouveau" (Université Laval, Quebec City, October 27–29, 2010), forthcoming.

53. Giuseppe Alberigo, "Transition to a New Age," in *History of Vatican II*, vol. 5, *The Council and the Transition*, ed. Joseph A. Komonchak (Maryknoll, NY: Orbis, 2005), 611.

54. On the hermeneutical issue of continuity/discontinuity in Benedict XVI, see Lieven Boeve, "'La vraie réception de Vatican II n'a pas encore commencè. Joseph Ratzinger, révélation et autorité de Vatican II," *Ephemerides Theologicae Lovanienses* 85/4 (2009): 305–39.

EPILOGUE

1. Thomas S. Kuhn, *The Structure of Scientific Revolutions* (Chicago: University of Chicago Press, 1962).

2. Giuseppe Alberigo, *La chiesa nella storia* (Brescia: Paideia, 1988), 218–39.

3. Richard John Neuhaus, "The Councils Called Vatican II," in Richard John Neuhaus, *The Catholic Moment: The Paradox of the Church in the Postmodern World* (San Francisco: Harper and Row, 1987), 61.

4. Concerning the almost classical division of the first decades of post–Vatican II into three different periods, see Hermann Josef Pottmeyer, "A New Phase in the Reception of Vatican II: Twenty Years of Interpretation of Vatican II," in *The Reception of Vatican II*, ed. Giuseppe Alberigo, Jean-Pierre Jossua, and Joseph A. Komonchak (Washington, DC: Catholic University of America Press, 1985), 27–43; Walter Kasper, "Die bleibende Herausforderung durch das II. Vatikanische Konzil. Zur Hermeneutik der Konzilsaussagen," in

Walter Kasper, *Die Kirche Jesu Christi. Schriften zur Ekklesiologie, I* (Walter Kasper Gesammelte Schriften, 11) (Freiburg: Herder, 2008), 200–211, esp. 200–201; Karl Lehmann, "Das II. Vatikanum—Ein Wegweiser. Verständnis—Rezeption—Bedeutung," in *Das Zweite Vatikanische Konzil und die Zeichen der Zeit heute*, ed. Peter Hünermann (Freiburg: Herder, 2006), 11–28, esp. 22–24.

5. See Massimo Faggioli, "Die kulturelle und politische Relevanz des II. Vatikanischen Konzils als konstitutiver Faktor der Interpretation," in *Exkommunikation oder Kommunikation? Der Weg der Kirche nach dem II. Vatikanum und die Pius-Brüder*, ed. Peter Hünermann (Freiburg: Herder, 2009), 153–74; Massimo Faggioli, "Vatican II Comes of Age," *The Tablet*, April 11, 2009, 16–17.

BIBLIOGRAPHY

HISTORY OF VATICAN II

Acerbi, Antonio. *Due ecclesiologie. Ecclesiologia giuridica e ecclesiologia di comunione nella Lumen gentium.* Bologna: EDB, 1975.

Alberigo, Giuseppe. *A Brief History of Vatican II.* Maryknoll, NY: Orbis, 2006. Originally published as *Breve storia del concilio Vaticano II* (Bologna: Il Mulino, 2005).

Alberigo, Giuseppe, ed. *History of Vatican II.* 5 vols. English version edited by Joseph A. Komonchak. Maryknoll, NY: Orbis, 1995–2006.

Alberigo, Giuseppe, and Franca Magistretti, eds. *Constitutionis dogmaticae Lumen gentium Synopsis historica.* Bologna: Istituto per le scienze religiose, 1975.

Alberigo, Giuseppe, and Alberto Melloni, eds. *Verso il concilio Vaticano II (1960–1962). Passaggi e problemi della preparazione conciliare.* Bologna: Il Mulino, 1993.

Bellitto, Christopher M. *Renewing Christianity: A History of Church Reform from Day One to Vatican II.* New York/Mahwah, NJ: Paulist Press, 2001.

Beozzo, José Oscar, ed. *Cristianismo e iglesias de América Latina en vísperas del Vaticano II.* San José, Costa Rica: Editorial DEI/CEHILA, 1992.

Burigana, Riccardo. *La Bibbia nel concilio. La redazione della costituzione Dei Verbum del Vaticano II.* Bologna: Il Mulino, 1998.

Le deuxième concile du Vatican (1959–1965). Rome: École Française de Rome; Paris: Diffusion de Boccard, 1989.

Doré, Joseph, and Alberto Melloni, eds. *Volti di fine Concilio. Studi di storia e teologia sulla conclusione del Vaticano II.* Bologna: Il Mulino, 2001.

Faggioli, Massimo. *Il vescovo e il concilio. Modello episcopale e aggiornamento al Vaticano II.* Bologna: Il Mulino, 2005.

Faggioli, Massimo, and Giovanni Turbanti, eds. *Il concilio inedito. Fonti del Vaticano II.* Bologna: Il Mulino, 2001.

Fattori, Maria Teresa, and Alberto Melloni, eds. *L'evento e le decisioni. Studi sulle dinamiche del concilio Vaticano II.* Bologna: Il Mulino, 1997.

———. *Experience, Organisations and Bodies at Vatican II.* Leuven: Bibliotheek van de Faculteit Godgeleerdheid, 1997.

Greiler, Alois. *Das Konzil und die Seminare. Die Ausbildung der Priester in der Dynamik des Zweiten Vatikanums.* Louvain-Paris-Dudley, MA: Peeters, 2003.

Indelicato, Antonino. *Difendere la dottrina o annunciare l'Evangelo. Il dibattito nella Commissione centrale preparatoria del Vaticano II.* Genoa: Marietti, 1992.

Kaufmann, Franz-Xaver, and Arnold Zingerle, eds. *Vatikanum II und Modernisierung. Historische, theologische und soziologische Perspektiven.* Paderborn: Schöningh, 1996.

Lamberigts, Mathijs, Claude Soetens, and Jan Grootaers, eds. *Les commissions conciliaires à Vatican II.* Louvain: Peeters, 1996.

Levillain, Philippe. *La mécanique politique de Vatican II. La majorité et l'unanimité dans un Concile.* Paris: Beauchesne, 1975.

McEnroy, Carmel. *Guests in Their Own House: The Women of Vatican II.* New York: Crossroad, 1996.

Melloni, Alberto, ed. *Vatican II in Moscow (1959–1962).* Leuven: Bibliotheek van de Faculteit Godgeleerdheid, 1997.

O'Malley, John W. *What Happened at Vatican II.* Cambridge, MA: Belknap Press, 2008.

Scatena, Silvia. *La fatica della libertà. L'elaborazione della dichiarazione Dignitatis humanae sulla libertà religiosa del Vaticano II*. Bologna: Il Mulino, 2003.

Turbanti, Giovanni. *Un concilio per il mondo moderno. La redazione della costituzione pastorale Gaudium et spes del Vaticano II*. Bologna: Il Mulino, 2000.

Velati, Mauro. *Una difficile transizione. Il cattolicesimo tra unionismo ed ecumenismo (1952–1964)*. Bologna: Il Mulino, 1996.

Wicks, Jared. "Six Texts by Prof. Joseph Ratzinger as *peritus* before and during Vatican Council II." *Gregorianum* 89/2 (2008): 233–311.

Wittstadt, Klaus, and Wim Verschooten, eds. *Der Beitrag der deutschsprachigen und osteuropäischen Länder zum zweiten vatikanischen Konzil*. Louvain: Peeters, 1996.

Wolf, Hubert, ed. *Die deutschsprachigen Länder und das II Vatikanum*. Paderborn: Schöningh, 2000.

JOURNALS, DIARIES, AND MEMOIRS

Camara, Helder. *Vaticano II: Correspondência conciliar. Circulares á família do São Joaquim*. Edited by Luiz Carlos Marques. Recife, Brazil: Instituto Dom Helder Camara-Editora Universitaria UFPE, 2004. Translated in French as *Lettres conciliaires, 1962–1965*, ed. José de Broucker (Paris: Cerf, 2006). Translated in Italian as *Roma, due del mattino. Lettere dal Concilio Vaticano II*, ed. Sandra Biondo (Cinisello Balsamo, Milan: San Paolo, 2008).

———. *Circulares Interconciliares*. Recife, Brazil: Companhia Editora de Pernambuco, 2008.

Chenu, Marie-Dominique. *Notes quotidiennes au Concile: Journal de Vatican II 1962–1963*. Edited by Alberto Melloni. Paris: Cerf, 1995.

Congar, Yves. *Mon journal du concile*. Edited by Éric Mahieu. Paris: Cerf, 2002.

Döpfner, Julius. *Tagebücher, Briefe und Notizen zum Zweiten Vatikanischen Konzil*. Edited by Guido Treffler. Regensburg: Schnell-Steiner, 2006.

Horton, Douglas. *Vatican Diary*. 4 vols. Philadelphia: United Church Press, 1964–66.

Lercaro, Giacomo. *Lettere dal Concilio: 1962–1965*. Edited by Giuseppe Battelli. Bologna: EDB, 1980.

Lubac, Henri de. *Carnets du Concile*. Edited by Loïc Figoureux. Paris: Cerf, 2007.

Philips, Gérard. *Carnets conciliaires de Mgr Gérard Philips, secrétaire adjoint de la Commission doctrinale*. Edited by Karim Schelkens and Leo Declerck. Louvain: Peeters, 2006.

Roncalli, Angelo Giuseppe (John XXIII). *Pater amabilis. Agende del pontefice, 1958–1963*. Edited by Mauro Velati. Bologna: Fondazione per le scienze religiose, 2007.

Rouquette, René. *La fin d'une chrétienté. Chroniques*. 2 vols. Paris: Cerf, 1968.

Rynne, Xavier [Francis X. Murphy]. *Vatican Council II*. Maryknoll, NY: Orbis Books, 1999.

Stacpoole, Alberic, ed. *Vatican II by those who were there*. Minneapolis, MN: Winston Press, 1986.

Tromp, Sebastian. *Diarium Secretarii Commissionis Theologicae Concilii Vaticani II—Konzilstagebuch mit Erläuterungen und Akten aus der Arbeit der Theologischen Kommission*. Edited by Alexandra von Teuffenbach. Rome: Pontificia Università Gregoriana, 2006.

Wiltgen, Ralph. *The Rhine Flows into the Tiber*. New York: Hawthorn Books, 1967; Rockford, IL: Tan Books, 1985.

COMMENTARIES

Barauna, Guilherme, ed. *La Chiesa del Vaticano II: studi e commenti intorno alla costituzione dommatica Lumen gentium.* Florence: Vallecchi, 1965.

———. *The Liturgy of Vatican II. A Symposium.* English translation edited by Jovian Lang. 2 vols. Chicago: Franciscan Herald Press, 1966.

———. *L'église dans le monde de ce temps. Ètudes et commentaires autour de la constitution pastorale Gaudium et spes de Vatican II.* Edition française dirigée par Henri Crouzel, Bruges: Desclée de Brouwer, 1967.

Bevans, Stephen B., and Jeffrey Gros. *Evangelization and Religious Freedom: Ad Gentes, Dignitatis Humanae.* New York/Mahwah, NJ: Paulist Press, 2009.

Cassidy, Edward. *Ecumenism and Interreligious Dialogue: Unitatis Redintegratio, Nostra Aetate.* New York/Mahwah, NJ: Paulist Press, 2005.

Confoy, Maryanne. *Religious Life and Priesthood: Perfectae Caritatis, Optatam Totius, Presbyterorum Ordinis.* New York/Mahwah, NJ: Paulist Press, 2008.

Congar, Yves, and Michel Peuchmaurd, eds. *L'Église dans le monde de ce temps.* Paris: Cerf, 1967.

Ferrone, Rita. *Liturgy: Sacrosanctum Concilium.* New York/Mahwah, NJ: Paulist Press, 2007.

Gaillardetz, Richard. *The Church in the Making: Lumen gentium, Christus Dominus, Orientalium Ecclesiarum.* New York/Mahwah NJ: Paulist Press, 2006.

Hilberath, Hans Jochen, and Peter Hünermann, eds. *Herders Theologischer Kommentar zum Zweiten Vatikanischen Konzil.* 5 vols. Freiburg: Herder, 2004–5.

191

Leckey, Dolores R. *The Laity and Christian Education: Apostolicam Actuositatem, Gravissimum Educationis.* New York/Mahwah, NJ: Paulist Press, 2006.

Philips, Gérard. *L'Église et son mystère au IIe Concile du Vatican. Histoire, text et commentaire de la constitution "Lumen gentium."* Paris: Desclée, 1966–68.

Tanner, Norman. *The Church and the World: Gaudium et Spes, Inter Mirifica.* New York/Mahwah, NJ: Paulist Press, 2005.

Vorgrimler, Herbert, ed. *Commentary on the Documents of Vatican II.* Translated by Lalit Adolphus, Kevin Smyth, and Richard Strachan. London: Burns & Oates; New York: Herder & Herder, 1967–69. Original published as *Lexikon Für Theologie und Kirche. Das Zweite Vatikanische Konzil: Konstitutionen, Dekrete, und Erklärungen. Lateinisch und Deutsch Kommentare.* 3 vols. (Freiburg: Herder, 1966–68).

Witherup, Ronald D. *Scripture: Dei Verbum.* New York/Mahwah, NJ: Paulist Press, 2006.

RECEPTION OF VATICAN II

Alberigo, Giuseppe, Jean-Pierre Jossua, and Joseph A. Komonchak, eds. *The Reception of Vatican II.* Washington, DC: Catholic University of America Press, 1987.

Autiero, Antonio, ed. *Herausforderung Aggiornamento: zur Rezeption Vaticanischen Konzils.* Altenberge: Oros, 2000.

Barth, Karl. *Ad Limina Apostolorum: An Appraisal of Vatican II.* Translated by Keith R. Crim. Richmond, VA: John Knox Press, 1968.

Bischof, Franz Xaver, and Stephan Leimgruber, eds. *Vierzig Jahre II. Vatikanum: zur Wirkungsgeschichte der Konzilstexte.* Würzburg: Echter, 2004.

Corecco, Eugenio. "Aspects of the Reception of Vatican II in the Code of Canon Law." In *The Reception of Vatican II*, edited by Giuseppe Alberigo, Jean-Pierre Jossua, and Joseph A. Komonchak, 249–96. Washington, DC: Catholic University of America Press, 1987.

Greeley, Andrew. *The Catholic Revolution: New Wine, Old Wineskins, and the Second Vatican Council.* Berkeley: University of California Press, 2004.

Greinacher, Norbert, and Hans Küng, eds. *Katholische Kirche, wohin? Wider den Verrat am Konzil.* Munich: Piper, 1986.

Hierold, Alfred E., ed. *Zweites Vatikanisches Konzil—Ende oder Anfang?* Münster: LIT, 2004.

Ivereigh, Austin, ed. *Unfinished Journey: The Church 40 Years after Vatican II.* New York-London: Continuum, 2003.

Latourelle, René, ed. *Vatican II: Assessment and Perspectives: Twenty-five Years After (1962–1987).* 3 vols. New York/Mahwah, NJ: Paulist Press, 1988–89.

Lefebvre, Marcel. *I Accuse the Council!* Kansas City, MO: Angelus Press, 2007 Originally published as *J'accuse le Concile!* Paris: Éditions Saint-Gabriel, 1976.

Lindbeck, George. *The Future of Roman Catholic Theology: Vatican II–Catalyst for Change.* Philadelphia: Fortress, 1970.

Massa, Mark S. *The American Catholic Revolution: How the Sixties Changed the Church Forever.* New York: Oxford University Press, 2010.

Melloni, Alberto, and Christoph Theobald, eds. *Vatican II: A Forgotten Future?* London: SCM Press, 2005.

Moorman, John. *Vatican II Observed: An Anglican Impression of Vatican II.* London: Catholic Book Club, 1967.

Noceti, Serena. "Un caso serio della recezione conciliare: donne e teologia." *Ricerche Teologiche* XIII/1 (2002): 211–24.

O'Collins, Gerald. *Living Vatican II: The 21st Council for the 21st Century.* New York/Mahwah, NJ: Paulist Press, 2006.

O'Connell, Timothy E., ed. *Vatican II and Its Documents: An American Reappraisal.* Wilmington, DE: Michael Glazier, 1986.

Orsy, Ladislas. *Receiving the Council: Theological and Canonical Insights and Debates.* Collegeville, MN: Liturgical Press, 2009.

Phan, Peter. "Reception of Vatican II in Asia: Historical and Theological Analysis." *Gregorianum* 83 (2002): 269–85.

Rahner, Karl. *The Church after the Council.* See esp. "The Council: A New Beginning." Translated by Davis C. Herron and Rodelinde Albrecht. New York: Herder and Herder, 1966. Originally published as *Das Konzil: Ein neuer Beginn* (Freiburg: Herder, 1966).

Richard, Lucien, with Daniel T. Harrington and John W. O'Malley, eds. *Vatican II, The Unfinished Agenda: A Look to the Future.* New York/Mahwah, NJ: Paulist Press, 1987.

Routhier, Gilles, *Vatican II. Herméneutique et reception.* Montreal: Fides, 2006.

Routhier, Gilles, ed. *Réceptions de Vatican II. Le concile au risque de l'histoire et des espaces humains.* Louvain: Peeters, 2004.

Routhier, Gilles, and Guy Jobin, eds. *L'Autorité et les Autorités. L'hermenéutique théologique de Vatican II.* Paris: Cerf, 2010.

Schatz, Werner, ed. *Was bedeutet das Zweite Vatikanische Konzil für uns?* Basel: Reinhardt, 1966.

Schultenover, David G., ed. *Vatican II: Did Anything Happen?* New York-London: Continuum, 2007.

Sullivan, Maureen. *The Road to Vatican II: Key Changes in Theology.* New York/Mahwah, NJ: Paulist Press, 2007.

Tracy, David, ed. *Toward Vatican III: The Work That Needs to Be Done.* Nijmegen, Netherlands: Concilium; New York: Seabury Press, 1978.

Wassilowsky, Günther, ed. *Zweites Vaticanum—Vergessene Anstöße, gegenwärtige Fortschreibungen.* Freiburg: Herder, 2004.

THEOLOGICAL INTERPRETATIONS OF VATICAN II

Alberigo, Giuseppe. *Transizione epocale. Studi sul Concilio Vaticano II*. Bologna: Il Mulino, 2009.

Amerio, Romano. *Iota Unum: A Study of Change in the Catholic Church in the XX Century*. Translated from the second Italian edition by John P. Parson. Kansas City, MO: Sarto House, 1996. First Italian edition, Milano: R. Ricciardi, 1985; second edition, 1986; third edition, 1989. French edition Paris: Nouvelles editions latines, 1987. Republished in Italy by two different publishers (Turin: Lindau, edited by Enrico Maria Radaelli, preface by Cardinal Dario Castrillon Hoyos, 2009; Verona: Fede e Cultura, 2009).

Bordeyne, Philippe, and Laurent Villemin, eds. *Vatican II et la théologie: Perspectives pour le XXIe siècle*. Paris: Cerf, 2006.

Bulman, Raymond F., and Frederick J. Parrella. *From Trent to Vatican II: Historical and Theological Perspectives*. New York: Oxford University Press, 2006.

Chenu, Marie-Dominique. "La fin de l'ère constantinienne." In *Un concile pour notre temps*, edited by Jean-Pierre Dubois-Dumee et al., 59–87. Paris: Cerf, 1961.

Congar, Yves. *Le Concile Vatican II. Peuple de Dieu et corps du Christ*. Paris: Beauchesne, 1984.

Dulles, Avery. *Models of the Church*. New York: Image/Doubleday, 2002.

———. "Vatican II: The Myth and the Reality." *America*, February 24, 2003, 7–11.

———. "Vatican II: Substantive Teaching." *America*, March 31, 2003, 14–17.

Faggioli, Massimo. "Concilio Vaticano II: bollettino bibliografico (2000–2002)." *Cristianesimo nella Storia* 24/2 (2003): 335–60.

————. "Concilio Vaticano II: bollettino bibliografico (2002–2005)." *Cristianesimo nella Storia* 26/3 (2005): 743–67.

————. "Council Vatican II: Bibliographical Overview 2005–2007." *Cristianesimo nella Storia* 29/2 (2008): 567–610.

————. "Council Vatican II: Bibliographical Overview 2007–2010." *Cristianesimo nella Storia* 32/2 (2010): 755–91.

Hünermann, Peter. "Der Text: Werden—Gestalt—Bedeutung. Eine Hermeneutische Reflexion." In *Herders Theologischer Kommentar zum Zweiten Vatikanischen Konzil*, edited by Hans Jochen Hilberath and Peter Hünermann, 5:5–101. Freiburg: Herder, 2004–5.

Kasper, Walter. *Theology and Church*. See especially "The Church as Universal Sacrament of Salvation." New York: Crossroad, 1989.

————. "On the Church: A Friendly Reply to Cardinal Ratzinger." *America* 184 (April 23–30, 2001): 8–14; originally published in *Stimmen der Zeit* 12 (December 2000), 795–804.

Komonchak, Joseph A. "Interpreting the Council." In *Being Right: Conservative Catholics in America*, edited by Mary Jo Weaver and R. Scott Appleby, 17–36. Bloomington: Indiana University Press, 1995.

————. "Riflessioni storiografiche sul Vaticano II come evento." In *L'evento e le decisioni. Studi sulle dinamiche del concilio Vaticano II*, edited by Maria Teresa Fattori and Alberto Melloni, 417–39. Bologna: Il Mulino, 1997.

————. "Augustine, Aquinas, or the Gospel *sine glossa*?" In *Unfinished Journey: The Church 40 Years after Vatican II. Essays for John Wilkins*, edited by Austin Ivereigh, 102–18. New York-London: Continuum, 2005.

————. "The Council of Trent at the Second Vatican Council." In *From Trent to Vatican II: Historical and Theological Perspectives*, edited by Raymond F. Bulman and Frederick

J. Parrella, 61–80. New York: Oxford University Press, 2006.

———. "Benedict XVI and the Interpretation of Vatican II." *Cristianesimo nella Storia* 28/2 (2007): 323–37.

———. "Novelty in Continuity. Pope Benedict's Interpretation of Vatican II." *America*, February 2, 2009, 10–16.

Lamb, Matthew L., and Matthew Levering, eds. *Vatican II: Renewal within Tradition*. Oxford–New York: Oxford University Press, 2008.

Legrand, Hervé-Marie. "Les éveques, les églises locales et l'église entiére. Evolutions institutionelles depuis Vatican II et chantiers actuels de recherche." *Revue de Sciences philosophiques et théologiques* 85 (2001): 461–509.

Lehmann, Karl. "Das II. Vatikanum—ein Wegweiser: Verständnis—Rezeption—Bedeutung." In *Das Zweite Vatikanische Konzil und die Zeichen der Zeit heute*, edited by Peter Hünermann, 11–26. Freiburg: Herder, 2006.

Lubac, Henri de. *Entretien Autour de Vatican II: Souvenirs et Réflexions*. Paris: Cerf, 1985.

Marchetto, Agostino. *Il Concilio ecumenico Vaticano II. Contrappunto per la sua storia*. Vatican City: Libreria Editrice Vaticana, 2005. Translated by Kenneth D. Whitehead as *The Second Vatican Ecumenical Council: A Counterpoint for the History of the Council* (Scranton, PA: University of Scranton Press, 2010).

Melloni, Alberto. "Breve guida ai giudizi sul Vaticano II." In *Chi ha paura del Vaticano II?* edited by Alberto Melloni and Giuseppe Ruggieri, 107–45. Rome: Carocci, 2009.

O'Malley, John. *Tradition and Transition: Historical Perspectives on Vatican II*. Wilmington, DE: Michael Glazier, 1989.

———. "The Style of Vatican II." *America*, February 24, 2003, 12–15.

————. "Vatican II: Official Norms." *America*, March 31, 2003, 11–14.

————. "Vatican II: Did Anything Happen?" *Theological Studies* 67 (2006): 3–33.

Ormerod, Neil. "Vatican II—Continuity or Discontinuity? Toward an Ontology of Meaning." *Theological Studies* 71 (2010): 609–36.

Pottmeyer, Hermann J. "A New Phase in the Reception of Vatican II: Twenty Years of Interpretation of the Council." In *The Reception of Vatican II*, edited by Giuseppe Alberigo, Jean-Pierre Jossua, and Joseph A. Komonchak, 27–43. Washington, DC: Catholic University of America Press, 1987.

————. *Towards a Papacy in Communion: Perspectives from Vatican Councils I and II.* Translated by Matthew J. O'Connell. New York: Crossroad, 1998.

Rahner, Karl. *Theological Investigations Vol. VI: Concerning Vatican II.* London-New York: Darton, Longman & Todd-Seabury Press, 1974.

Ratzinger, Joseph (Benedict XVI). *Theological Highlights of Vatican II.* Translated by Henry Traub, SJ, Gerard C. Thormann, and Werner Barzel. New York: Paulist Press, 1966. Reprinted with an introduction by Thomas P. Rausch. New York/Mahwah, NJ: Paulist Press, 2009.

————. *Dogma und Verkündigung.* See esp. the epilogue, "Zehn Jahre nach Konzilsbeginn—wo stehen wir?" Munich-Freiburg: Wewel, 1973.

————. *Principles of Catholic Theology: Building Stones for a Fundamental Theology.* San Francisco: Ignatius Press, 1987.

————. "L'ecclesiologia della costituzione Lumen Gentium," in *Il Concilio Vaticano II: recezione e attualità alla luce del giubileo*, edited by Rino Fisichella (Cinisello B.: San Paolo, 2000), 66–81.

————. Christmas Address to the Roman Curia, December 22, 2005. In *Insegnamenti di Benedetto XVI*, vol. 1 (2005). Vatican City: Libreria Editrice Vaticana, 2006, 1018–32. English translation at http://www.vatican.va/holy_father/benedict_xvi/speeches/2005/december/documents/hf_ben_xvi_spe_20051222_roman-curia_en.html.

Ruggieri, Giuseppe. "Ricezioni e interpretazioni del Vaticano II. Le ragioni di un dibattito." In *Chi ha paura del Vaticano II?* edited by Alberto Melloni and Giuseppe Ruggieri, 17–44. Rome: Carocci, 2009.

Rush, Ormond. *Still Interpreting Vatican II: Some Hermeneutical Principles*. New York/Mahwah, NJ: Paulist Press, 2004.

Schillebeeckx, Edward. *The Real Achievement of Vatican II*. Translated by H. J. J. Vaughan. New York: Herder and Herder, 1966.

Schloesser, Stephen. "Against Forgetting: Memory, History, Vatican II." *Theological Studies* 67 (2006): 275–319.

Theobald, Christoph. *La réception du concile Vatican II, I. Accéder à la source*. Paris: Cerf, 2009.

————. *"Dans les traces..." de la constitution "Dei Verbum" du concile Vatican II. Bible, théologie et pratiques de lecture*. Paris: Cerf, 2009.

————, ed. *Vatican II sous le regard des historiens*. Paris: Centre Sèvres—Faculté jésuites de Paris, 2006.

Wicks, Jared. *Doing Theology*. New York/Mahwah NJ: Paulist Press, 2009.

green press
INITIATIVE